Master Classes in Education Series

Working with Adolescents: Constructing Identity

John Head

 The Falmer Press

(A member of the Taylor & Francis Group)
London • Washington, D.C.

UK   Falmer Press, 1 Gunpowder Square, London EC4A 3DE
USA   Falmer Press, Taylor & Francis Inc., 1900 Frost Road, Suite 101, Bristol,
          PA 19007

First published in 1997

**A catalogue record for this book is available from the British
Library**

**Library of Congress Cataloging-in-Publication Data are available on
request**

ISBN 0 7507 0730 5 cased
ISBN 0 7507 0643 0 paper

Cover design by Caroline Archer

Typeset in 11/13pt Garamond and printed by
Graphicraft Typesetters Ltd., Hong Kong.

Working with Adolescents

Master Classes in Education Series

Series Editors: John Head, School of Education, Kings College, University of London and Ruth Merttens, School of Teaching Studies, University of North London

Working with Adolescents: Constructing Identity
John Head *Kings College, University of London*

Testing: Friend or Foe? The Theory and Practice of Assessment and Testing
Paul Black *Kings College, University of London*

Doing Research/Reading Research: A Mode of Interrogation for Education
Andrew Brown and Paul Dowling *both of the Institute of Education, University of London*

Educating the Other: Gender, Power and Schooling
Carrie Paechter *School of Education, The Open University*

Contents

Preface

It has become a feature of our times that an initial qualification is no longer seen to be adequate for life-long work within a profession and programmes of professional development are needed. Nowhere is the need more clear than with respect to education, where changes in the national schooling and assessment system, combined with changes in the social and economic context, have transformed our professional lives.

The series, *Master Classes in Education*, is intended to address the needs of professional development, essentially at the level of taught masters degrees. Although aimed primarily at teachers and lecturers, it is envisaged that the books will appeal to a wider readership, including those involved in professional educational management, health promotion and youth work. For some, the texts will serve to up-date their knowledge. For others, they may facilitate career reorientation by introducing, in an accessible form, new areas of expertise or knowledge.

The books are overtly pedagogical, providing a clear track through the topic by means which make it possible to gain a sound grasp of the whole field. Each book familiarizes the reader with the vocabulary and the terms of discussion and provides a concise overview of recent research and current debates in the area. While it is obviously not possible to deal with every aspect in depth, a professional who has read the book should be able to feel confident that they have covered the major areas of content, and discussed the different issues at stake. The books are also intended to convey a sense of the future direction of the subject and its points of growth or change.

In each subject area the reader is introduced to different perspectives and to a variety of readings of the subject under consideration. Some of the readings may conflict, others may be compatible but distant. Different perspectives may well give rise to different lexicons and different bibliographies, and the reader is always alerted to these differences. The variety of frameworks within which each topic can be construed is then a further source of reflective analysis.

The authors in this series have been carefully selected. Each person is an experienced professional, who has worked in that area of education as a practitioner and also addressed the subject as both a researcher and theoretician. Drawing upon both pragmatic and the theoretical aspects of their experience, they are able to take a reflective view while preserving a sense of what occurs, and what is possible, at the level of practice.

Working with Adolescents: Constructing Identity

This book, the first in the series, takes a broad view of the field, providing a theoretical overview, reviewing the findings of recent and relevant research and dealing with some of the practical issues of living and working with adolescents. It is interdisciplinary, using notions derived from psychology, notably that of personal identity, but at the same time recognizing the importance of the social context within which identity comes to be constructed. The author is aware of the dangers of producing a unified subject, a universal 'adolescent'. The diversity of adolescent experience and practice is addressed through a consistent awareness of the actual and specific differences, including gender, which divide adolescents from each other as well as from the 'adult' world.

It is often the case that those writing in a reflective capacity about a field as diverse and as riven by dispute as this one, take up a particular position and read all research and practice from this perspective. John Head avoids such particularity, displaying unswerving faithfulness to the intentions of those writers which he discusses. The text, accompanied by suggestions for further reading, provides a good understanding of theorists such as Freud, Erikson, Marcia and Gilligan. The treatment provides the reader with the opportunity to engage with different perspectives in the confidence that the inevitable simplification does not lead to distortion.

Adolescence may be defined as that period of our lives in which the question of identity assumes momentous proportions. As the writer Annie Dillard (1987) puts it,

> So this was adolescence. Is this how the people around me had died on their feet — inevitably, helplessly? Perhaps their own selves had eclipsed the sun for so many years the world shriveled around them, and when at last their inescapable orbits had passed through these dark egoistic years it was too late, they had adjusted.

Adolescence is a complex and important construction, about which we learn not only through reflection but through our own experiences. Always aware of these pragmatic considerations, John Head never lets us forget what we do, as well as why we do it, is theoretically grounded.

Ruth Merttens
Joint Series Editor

Acknowledgments

Three people read a complete draft of the manuscript and made most useful suggestions for improvements. Professor Ruth Merttens of North London University is the Joint Editor of the series *Master Classes in Education* and she looked at how well the draft fitted in with the aims for the series. I have had the good fortune of having Dr. Krzysztof Blusz of the University of Lodz in Poland working alongside me in London and have benefitted from his detailed knowledge of identity theory. Ms Lynette Rentoul, of the Department of Nursing Studies in King's College, London, has had experience of working with adolescents within institutions for family reasons or because of physical or mental problems, and she provided me with insights gained from such work. In addition, Dr. Carrie Paechter of The Open University has read and commented on part of the manuscript. Ms Jane Jones, of the School of Education at King's College, London, gave me valuable help with respect to counselling issues.

There are many others who I cannot name individually. The need for this book became clear to me through teaching on a variety of taught master degree courses. I gained immensely from the discussions which I have had with the students coming from different backgrounds such as teachers, clergy and those working in health promotion and education. My understanding of adolescence has been enriched through undertaking empirical work in schools and I must thank the teachers and students who had to put up with me interrupting their routines.

Acknowledgements

Chapter 1

Introduction: Perspectives on Adolescence

The common dictionary definition of adolescence, as the phase of life between childhood and adulthood, gives no hint of the concerns and controversy which surround it. Within our culture adolescence is often seen to possess some unique quality which distinguishes it from other parts of the life-span. There is less agreement about the nature of this quality.

Often there is a very negative image. In part this comes from tabloid newspaper headlines about drugs, sex and crime. Tales are told of insubordinate youth in schools and anti-social behaviour outside school. Parents tell of happy and sociable children becoming sullen and uncommunicative teenagers. Given this picture we might think that one needs considerable tolerance and skill to work successfully with adolescents.

There are conflicting stories. Many adults will recall adolescence as a vitally important time in which life-long friendships were established and life-long values and interests emerged. Adolescence can be a time of enthusiasms and idealism and many teachers will testify to the exhilaration which can be experienced in working alongside young people.

Making sense of these conflicting images might be facilitated by seeing how our notions of adolescence as a special phase of life, one of storm and stress, evolved over the last two centuries.

Storm and Stress?

In pre-industrial societies children help in the home and with work as soon as they are able and, in so doing, become quietly initiated into adulthood. Puberty is often marked by some initiation ceremony, echoed by the Bar Mitzvah and the First Communion in our society. Some change in behaviour is expected after this initiation. For example, boys who previously lived with other children and the women may now be expected to keep the company of the adult men. The extended period of adolescence, as we know it, is collapsed in these societies into the short period of initiation, so that someone would be perceived as child one day and as an adult the next.

Even in such societies some tension between youth and adults was reported. In Classical Greece it was lamented that the youth of the day did not properly respect their elders and in 1590 the Recorder of London commented on the ill behaviour of gangs of youths in the city. In 1517 a riot among apprentices in London led to 300 arrests and one death. If in Tudor England the family and community could not provide for all in the home then it was expected that it would be the young men who would travel in search of employment. There is the old adage that 'girls take root while boys take flight'. The existence of a nomadic population, dependent on casual employment, charity, or *in extremis* petty crime, for survival gave cause for concern. It might be noted, however, that the comments were solely about the social behaviour of a sub-group within society and no attempt was made to engage with the minds of individual youths.

The big change came with the Romantic movement in Europe, leading to the observation that 'The adolescent was invented at the same time as the steam-engine' (Musgrove, 1964). Rousseau addressed the condition of childhood but Goethe had a greater influence with respect to adolescence. In 1774 he wrote *The Sufferings of Young Werther* which described a sensitive youth experiencing suicidal despair in facing the adult world. The book was an instant success and legend has it that there was a rash of similar suicides across Europe. A whole genre of similar literature then developed, being given the name Sturm und Drang after the title of a play by one of Goethe's associates, Friedrich von Klinger.

It is important to note that Goethe did not give a totally negative account of adolescence. Towards the end of his life, in conversation with Johann Eckermann in 1828, he credited his continuing creativity to having experienced 'repeated puberty'. His thesis was that adolescence might be marked by emotional turbulence but this provided the source for artistic achievement. Certainly, introspection became commonplace among the later Romantics, as demonstrated by Wordsworth in his autobiographical account, *The Prelude*, with the sub-title *Growth of a Poet's Mind*. It is not clear from these writings the extent to which the descriptions of adolescence were meant to describe the experience of all young people or solely those of an artistic temperament.

The first major psychological study of adolescence, by Stanley Hall in 1904, reinforced the notion of a time of storm and stress for all adolescents. Hall's writing combined a curious mix of careful detailed descriptions with strange explanatory models. He was strongly influenced by Darwin, and argued that each person's life-span recapitulates the evolutionary history of mankind. Within this bizarre theory adolescence corresponded to time when people became civilized, and there was tension between primitive desires and the influence of a civilized society.

A similar argument was made more cogently within psychoanalysis, when Freud moved the conflict between God and the Devil from outside a person to it being something within the mind. He postulated a struggle between the primitive instincts of the id and the moral conscience of the super-ego, with the ego, the more conscious and rational part of the mind, holding the balance. This model has been memorably likened to that of a sex-crazed monkey being in a perpetual struggle with a maiden aunt while the fight is refereed by a nervous bank clerk.

Figure 1: *Percentage of age cohorts in England and Wales convicted or cautioned for an indictable offence in 1993*

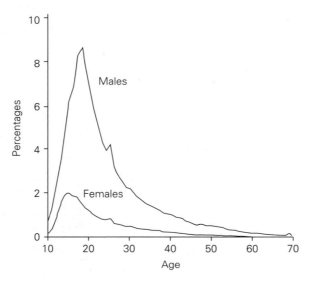

Source: *Social Trends,* 1995. Crown Copyright 1995. Reproduced by permission of the Controller of HMSO and of the Office for National Statistics.

Sigmund Freud did not pay much attention to adolescence, arguing that problems at this time of life were simply the continuation of problems unresolved in childhood. His daughter, Anna Freud, in her book *The Ego and the Mechanisms of Defence* published in 1937, took a different line. She argued that the child by the age of about six or seven has established a *modus vivendi* allowing it to cope successfully with the next phase of childhood, the so-called latency period, in which the child enjoys a time of psychic stability. However, the growth of sexual feelings accompanying puberty strengthens the id, so that for a while the psychic balance is disturbed. Consequently, according to this argument, there will inevitably be a period of storm and stress before a new equilibrium is established. Further writing within the psychoanalytical tradition, such as Blos (1962), has reinforced the notion of adolescent trauma, with him describing it as a time of a second individualization, completing the process which commenced at birth.

Reference has been made to the evidence for adolescent trauma. The story is confused. On many headings, such as that of physical health, it is a relatively trouble free time, with menstrual difficulties among the girls being the main exception. Other indicators tell a different story. Examination of *Figure 1*, showing the crime figures in Britain in 1993, show that the occurrence of indictable offences peaks strongly with males at about the age of eighteen, when over 8 per cent of the age cohort are convicted or cautioned. There is a much smaller peak with females at about the age of fifteen. Overall, 26 per cent of all known offenders are aged under eighteen.

With young women other indicators, notably eating disorders, are worrying. It is difficult to provide a precise figure for the incidence of such problems,

Figure 2:   *Suicide rates: by gender and age in England and Wales 1971–1992*

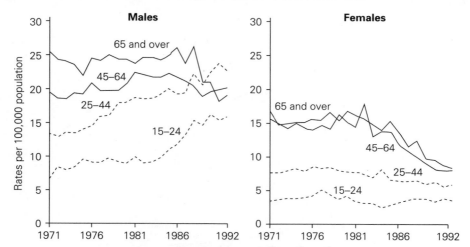

Source: Social Trends, 1995. Crown Copyright 1995. Reproduced by permission of the Controller of HMSO and of the Office for National Statistics.

as only the most severe cases are likely to be reported. The two commonest explanations for these disorders are a wish to appear very slim, as such a body shape is deemed attractive, and in some cases a wish to reverse the physical symptoms of puberty, specifically menstruation.

Some of the indicators show historical changes. Suicide rates have traditionally been low among this age group, but *Figure 2* shows that between 1971 and 1992 the rate for males aged 15 to 24 more than doubled, from about 7 per 100 000 of the population, to over 15, whereas among older males the rate decreased. There was no corresponding increase in suicide rates among young women where the figures have remained at just under 4 per 100 000.

Other evidence is open to conflicting interpretations. In recent years the number of pupils permanently excluded from our schools has increased, but this finding can be seen either as evidence of an increasing number of young people behaving badly, or as evidence that with the increasing competition among schools they are less willing to tolerate disruptive students. We also know that the use of cannabis among young people over the age of fifteen has now almost become the norm. How alarming we find that statistic

Activity
Recall your own experience of adolescence, and that of your contemporaries, in order to judge the extent that it was a time of storm and stress. It might help this task to make separate lists of the positive and negative aspects which you recall. The items listed form an agenda which should be addressed somewhere in this book. How is your list affected by your gender, race or class?

depends upon our beliefs about the likely dangers coming from the use of that drug.

The Essential Tasks of Adolescence

What emerges from this data is a complex and, to some extent, a contradictory picture which needs careful analysis to provide understanding. We must look beyond the too prevalent media scare stories to gain such understanding.

The weight of contemporary psychological opinion is that adolescence is not unique in being a time of extraordinary stress. However, each phase of life tends to present a specific set of stressors. A young adult coping with the demands of work and raising a family may envy the apparent care-free life of the adolescent. An older adult, who may be lonely now the children have grown up and left home, may envy those who have a young family. According to the criteria we select it is possible to make a case for any phase of life to storm and stress.

Adolescents have to cope with a number of tasks. Individually, the central task is to achieve a sense of personal identity and that concept, which is developed in the next chapter, provides an explanatory thread which then runs through the whole book. Achieving the autonomy necessary to become adult demands a change in the relationships with parents and teachers. The loosening of the ties with adult authority figures is compensated for by increased importance of relations with peers. The strength of the peer group influence can be positive, many adults testify to the value of friendships established in youth, but can also lead anti-social gang behaviour. A further complicating factor comes in the establishing of sexual relationships. Finally, adolescents as a social group occupy an ambiguous position in our society.

Given this agenda, of handling issues of identity, autonomy and changing relationships, it may be surprising that in general adolescents cope so well, without much trauma (Murray and Dawson, 1983; Davis, 1990). Coleman provides explanation terms of a focal model (Coleman, 1974; Coleman and Hendry, 1990). He suggests that adolescents cope by tackling the issues one at a time, and only after one has been resolved is the next addressed. In this fashion the stress at any given time is manageable. Obviously, the exact sequence depends on the individual, but his findings, as shown in *Figure 3*, suggests that among boys the biggest anxiety at the age of eleven is about the potential of heterosexual activity; for boys of fourteen and fifteen it is about rejection by the peer group; and at seventeen the biggest problem tends to be about relations with parents.

It is an open question whether adolescents face a more difficult task in growing into adulthood nowadays compared to the recent past. What is beyond dispute is that they are having to enter into a society which is undergoing rapid change. There is a loss of stability and certainty. Both marriages and employment, the two two key foundations to adult life, have become

Figure 3:   Sources of anxiety among boys

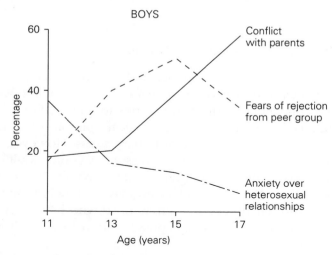

Source: COLEMAN (1974), as reproduced in COLEMAN, J.C. and HENDRY, L. (1990) *The Nature of Adolescence*, London: Routledge.

less secure. Under these circumstances we should at least recognize the magnitude of the challenges adolescents face.

Chapter Summary

- Although adolescents have long attracted adverse comment there is little historical evidence for there being an inevitable and universal period of crisis at this phase of life.
- A more balanced view would be to argue that adolescence poses a set of developmental tasks in moving from childhood into adulthood. Often these tasks are resolved without too much trauma.
- It is an open question whether the experience of adolescence is generally becoming more difficult nowadays, but the widespread instability with respect to employment and marriage poses problems.
- Some indicators, such as the increased suicide rate among young men, should alert us to the problems some adolescents face.

Further Reading

COLEMAN, J.C. and HENDRY, L. (1990) *The Nature of Adolescence*, London: Routledge.
COFFIELD, F., BORRILL, C. and MARSHALL, S. (1986) *Growing Up at the Margins*, Milton Keynes: Open University Press.

These two books have been chosen as they are in contrast and complement each other. The first volume provides a comprehensive and balanced psychological overview. The second book gives a vivid account of one ethnographic study.

Chapter 2

Acquiring a Sense of Identity

The concept of adolescent identity development has entered public consciousness for two reasons: it can be described in an accessible way and it accords with the experience of many people. The difficulties arise in academic psychology with issues of definition and the scope of the concept.

In everyday terms the argument is that children are largely defined by the significant adults in their life, but in adolescence they have to make a series of self-defining choices to allow them to function as autonomous adults.

The social class of children is that of their parents. They live where their parents choose to live and go to the school arranged by the parents. In school their actions are largely controlled by teachers. At home, in their leisure time and holidays, their activities are promoted and constrained by the parents. In becoming adult they have to sort out a number of issues. Most obviously they have to start on a career, a process which may start midway through secondary schooling, through the choice of school subjects for study. Eventually, they will leave home and have to build up their own social life. Before entering a long-term partnership they need to know what type of person they can effectively relate to, both in terms of their own sexual orientation, and also how they relate socially with other people. A further requirement is to settle on a desired life-style, a term which embraces such abstract notions as beliefs and values, and such practical matters as whether one lives in a city or the country and how leisure time might be spent.

It is clear that not any set of decisions will do. They have to be grounded in some realism. It would not be helpful for someone who is achieving poorly in academic work to aim to study medicine. There has to be a realistic assessment of one's abilities and interests and match these with a realistic sense of what different options will involve. Equally, a sense of identity will only work if it is coherent. It would not help an adolescent to decide on a career involving a lot of travel away from home and at the same time wanting a life-style centred around being at home with the family all the time.

Recognizing these requirements we can see why identity formation is centred in adolescence. It is unlikely that children will possess either the self-knowledge, or the knowledge of the wider world, to be able to make realistic matches between self and society. But it is also true that unless this process of making self-defining choices is undertaken in the adolescent years then the transition to adulthood will be problematic.

Although there is widespread consensus that the principal psychological task for the adolescent is to achieve a sense of personal identity there is no corresponding consensus about what precisely is meant by the term.

A Matter of Definition

There are two factors which can confuse us about identity. The first problem is that the word has been extended by analogy from relating to something about an individual to something about a social group of people. We can find, for example, reference to *corporate identity* or *national identity*. Erikson, the founding father of work on personal identity, talked of it describing simultaneously samenesses and differences. By the former he was referring to an intrapersonal coherence and consistency, without which an individual could not function effectively. By the latter he meant that someone's sense of identity distinguishes them from other people, it is a point of difference. By analogy a social group may possess shared values and beliefs, which confers a sameness, and at the same time members of this group feel different from other people. Like most analogies it breaks down if pushed too far. With personal identity we are interested in the psychodynamics of the individual which are qualitatively different from the social dynamics of the group.

Secondly, the use of terminology is inconsistent. Sometimes the expression *social identity* is used with reference to sub-groups in society, often defined with respect to class, race or gender, a concern with populations rather than individuals. In other words, it is seen as a part of anthropology or sociology, rather than psychology. Sometimes the terms refer to the idea of the social construction of identity, in which the development of individual identity is examined in terms of social interactions experienced by that person. The former possibility is outside the scope of this book. The notion of social construction is relevant, as clearly our self-concept will be influenced by what we believe others perceive about us. But even the social construction thesis can ignore the essential psychology, in seeing an individual passively being shaped by social forces, and not recognizing that people are reflexive beings who interpret what others do and say. The essential problem of this imprecise terminology is that a reader can pick up two books with a similar title, both containing the word identity, but find that they differ totally in approach and content.

Assuming that we confine our attention to the field of personal identity we still encounter a lack of a precise definition. Erikson, who combined the appeal of taking a broad view of human development with a failure to provide precise definitions, was the first culprit. Consider this definition: 'A sense of identity means being at one with oneself as one grows and develops: it also means, at the same time, a sense of affinity with a community's sense of being at one with its future as well as its history or mythology' (Erikson, 1974, pp. 27–8). This passage, which rewards a second reading, demonstrates the richness and complexity of his ideas. But it provides a definition which is almost impossible to operationalize.

He recognized the problem, and said of himself, 'I came to psychology from art, which may explain, if not justify, the fact that at times the reader will find me painting contexts and backgrounds where he would rather have me point to facts and concepts' (Erikson, 1950, p. 14).

One writer, Bourne (1978), has identified no less than seven aspects within Erikson's notion of identity:

- genetic; ego identity can be seen as an outcome of childhood, and the success or failure in dealing with earlier developmental tasks;
- adaptive; it is an adaptive response to the social environment, which involves having a realistic view of the world;
- structural; the possibility of identity diffusion, or breakdown (Breakwell, 1986), implies the existence of a structure which should possess resilience;
- dynamic; identity mediates between self and other and also between the id and the super-ego, identity formation is an active process;
- subjective; it helps one feel at home with oneself, that one can live with oneself;
- psychological reciprocity; the individual has to develop a reciprocal relationship with others, in contrast to childhood dependence;
- existential; identity provides a sense of meaning to self and the world, and successful living involves choice.

Others have attempted to be more succinct. Kroger (1996) defines identity as a 'balance between that which is taken to be the self and that considered to be the other'. My main reservation is that the word 'balance' is clearly crucial, but is itself vague. Adams (1992) is more precise in suggesting that 'Identity is conceptualized as an organized, self-regulatory psychic structure that requires the developmental distinction between the inner self and the outer world'. This description has appeal but we may prefer a briefer working definition.

Psychologists have learnt to work with descriptors which are used because they seem to work in operation, in bringing coherence to evidence and, crucially, in predicting outcomes. Identity theory must be judged on this basis and from my experience it stands up to the test. It allowed me to interpret data gathered from a large scale survey of adolescents (Head, 1980 and 1985). Furthermore, it has proved illuminating in counselling young adults who, in essence, are experiencing difficulties through failing to make identity choices, or the right choices, in adolescence.

In this situation we use a working definition, because it appears to have utility, but should remain open to possibility that subsequent experience may demand revision or the abandoning of the concept. My suggestion is that we might define identity development as *the process of making choices which allow one to live effectively as an adult* and identity itself is a *functional life script*. This definition is not meant to imply that adulthood will be free from the need to redefine oneself, merely that the young person has a life script which is adequate to take one forward into early adulthood.

Bournes' analysis indicates that any brief definition will be incomplete, but much of the essential message is carried within the two operational definitions proposed here. The idea of 'making choices' indicates that identity achievement is an active process, requiring the effort of the individual, and is not something which occurs spontaneously with maturation. The words 'effectively' and 'functional' are more tricky as they carry a normative tone, but they refer to the need for realism and coherence in a sense of identity. Finally, the notion of the life script carries the two-way image, that identity is created by the individual, who writes the script, but also controls the individual, who uses the script to guide actions. With this working definition in place we can explore in more detail the work of Erikson and his followers.

Erikson's Model

Prior to the work of Erik Erikson (1902–94) the word identity was rarely used in psychology, but in the 1960s, after his earlier books had become influential best-sellers, terms like 'identity crisis' passed into everyday speech. Rarely has one psychologist become so immediately and completely associated with a publicly known concept. This influence is even more surprising when we recall that he had no formal training in psychology. He trained as a Montessori teacher and taught in a small, private school in Vienna, with which Anna Freud was associated. Through this experience he became acquainted with Anna and Sigmund Freud. In 1933 he emigrated to the United States and working as a child psychoanalyst went on to hold senior positions in a number of institutions, including Harvard, Yale and Berkeley, prior to his retirement in 1970.

In a series of books, starting with *Childhood and Society* (Erikson, 1950), he elaborated his model of personal development incorporating the concept of identity. Essentially, he saw development occurring through a series of eight stages. These stages are seen to be hierarchical and possess an inner logic, so only after a satisfactory outcome at one stage can an individual cope effectively with the next.

Most developmental models assume that although individuals follow the same invariant route they can travel at their own pace. Cognitive psychologists, for example, would accept the notion that an exceptional child aged ten might display the thinking abilities of the average fifteen-year-old, in fact that is precisely what an IQ score of 150 would mean. Erikson's epigenesis of personality, to use his language, is not so open to variation. He assumed that certain biological and social determinants will ensure that each of the eight psychosocial stages will be faced in a particular phase of life.

The biological factor is particularly relevant to identity, as it is in adolescence, after the individual has experienced puberty and acquired the capacity to be sexually active, that the issues of sexuality become important. The social influences on adolescents involve gaining independence from the family and relying more on friends of one's own choice. In addition, the ending of compulsory schooling forces the adolescent to confront vocational choices. For these reasons Erikson saw identity formation as being an inevitable task of adolescence, although some elements, for example a sense of gender identity, would usually be in place long before adolescence.

Each of the eight stages presents what Erikson, borrowing the language of psychoanalysis, called a *crisis*, which has to be resolved before progressing further. The choice of the word crisis can be confusing as it implies an abrupt and traumatic event. As noted in the first chapter, the majority of adolescents do not experience too much trauma. Erikson subsequently softened the terminology by talking about a 'normative crisis', yet the confusion remains, and if the word crisis is to be retained it should be seen as a technical term in this context. The point he was trying to make is that each phase of life presents psychological challenges, and it would be an error for adults to see childhood and adolescence as completely untroubled and carefree times.

Erikson identified the eight psychosocial crises as being:

1   *Trust versus Mistrust* This stage occurs in early infancy and is seen to involve a crucial relationship with the mother. At this stage the child, through dependency on the mother, learns to have confidence in the benign quality of the external world.

2   *Autonomy versus Doubt* This stage corresponds to the psychoanalytical muscular-anal stage of early childhood in which the infant has to assume some control of itself and not depend totally on others. A successful outcome allows the child to develop some self-confidence.

3   *Initiative versus Guilt* At this stage the child has to learn to do things without being told, the child learns to accept responsibility for actions and the consequences.

4   *Industry versus Inferiority* The school environment provides a competitive situation in which the child has to develop the capacity to do well at school work and at the same time develop friendships with peers. Although this stage corresponds to the psychoanalytical concept of latency, Erikson saw it as more dynamic and challenging than the older term implies.

5   *Identity versus Role Confusion* If in adolescence a sense of identity does not emerge the individual will be confused in making decisions affecting adult life. Such confusion may be marked by the making of rash choices or by refusing to face the necessity of making choices.

6   *Intimacy versus Isolation* Only after a firm sense of personal identity has been acquired, he argued, can the young adult enter a truly intimate relationship with another. Without this sense of identity the

individual will lack the confidence to make a commitment and a partner will find it difficult to relate to someone who lacks consistency.

7   *Generativity versus Stagnation* Whether adulthood is spent profit-
ably depends on the possession of worthwhile goals. These meet the
need to be needed and involve going beyond one's own immediate
gratification. He saw the critical goals relating to work, the establishment of a family, and the possession sense of purpose in life.

8   *Integrity versus Despair* In old age one is apt to look back and
question the values of one's life and a sense of integrity is needed
to give it all some shape and purpose. Some way of facing inevitable
death has to be found.

Erikson took the first three or four stages from mainstream psychoanalytical literature and it is with stages five and six of his model that his
own voice speaks most clearly. Thus he wrote:

> But in puberty and adolescence all samenesses and continuities relied on
> earlier are more or less questioned again, because of a rapidity of body
> growth which equals that of early childhood, and because of the new addi-
> tion of genital maturity. The growing and developing youths, faced with this
> physiological revolution within them, and with the tangible adult tasks ahead
> of them are now primarily concerned with what they appear to be in the
> eyes of others as compared with what they feel they are, and with the ques-
> tion how to connect roles and skills cultivated earlier with occupational
> prototypes of the day. . . . The danger of this stage is role confusion. Where
> this is based on a strong doubt about one's sexual identity delinquent and
> outright psychotic episodes are not uncommon . . . In most instances, how-
> ever, it is the inability to settle to an occupational identity which disturbs
> young people. (1950, p. 235)

Erikson mentioned two of the main areas in which he saw identity
manifesting itself. The references to sexuality and occupational identity clearly
echo Freud, who suggested that happiness came from *Lieben und Arbeiten*,
love and work. Despite that claim Freud himself did not develop ideas on
the role of work in adult life, and Erikson's emphasis on the crucial importance
of what he called vocational identity, in the socialization of adolescents and
self-esteem of adults, established a new theme within psychology.

On sexuality Erikson's position is more open to criticism. He talked
of adolescent 'bisexual confusion' being resolved in the establishment of a
secure heterosexual relationship. It is hard to resist the conclusion that his
value judgments intruded into his descriptions at this point. There is no
empirical evidence which shows that concern about sexual identity specifically
leads to delinquent and psychotic episodes. Equally, there is no reason to
see all bisexual and homosexual behaviour as immature or destructive and
heterosexual behaviour as being inherently better for all.

Although Erikson attributed identity formation to adolescence he was not suggesting that other phases of life were unimportant to identity. Earlier childhood experiences would create the various elements of personality which had to be integrated into a coherent identity in adolescence. Adulthood might involve some return to identity confusion, particularly if there were a major change in life, such as redundancy or divorce. His argument was simply that in adolescence the establishment of an identity was necessarily and properly the key issue. He also argued that adolescents need a moratorium, a time to explore possibilities without for the moment having to commit themselves to a particular course, and that society should allow adolescents time and space for this moratorium to occur.

He tried to set self development within a social context, witness his shift from Freud's description of *psychosexual* development to his own of *psychosocial* development. The appeal of this element of his thinking is that it avoids the trap often attributed to psychologists of displaying what Jacoby (1975) called 'social amnesia', the failure to recognize social influences on the individual psyche. Erikson (1968) suggested, 'One methodological precondition, then, for grasping identity would be a psychoanalysis sophisticated enough to include the environment; the other would be a social psychology which is psychoanalytically sophisticated' (p. 24).

Whatever our criticisms of Erikson might be, and some of these will be discussed later in this chapter, his work was crucial. One of his limitations was that he essentially developed a theoretical model and did not say how it might prove useful in practice. It was left to others, notably Marcia, to develop practical ways of studying personal identity.

Marcia's Identity Statuses

In the late 1950s and early 1960s a variety of paper-and-pencil tests were developed to test people's identity development. In general, these proved unsatisfactory. The breakthrough came when James Marcia (1966) generated a new model which clarified the situation. His ideas have subsequently been extended and modified in later papers, for example, Marcia (1976 and 1980).

He identified two key processes occurring in identity development. First, it was necessary for the individual to actively explore the possibilities, a process involving the matching self-knowledge with knowledge of the world. Still working within the paradigm and language of psychoanalysis, Marcia described this process as 'undergoing crisis'. The second process involves making decisions, or what Marcia called 'commitment'. Sooner or later, the adolescent has to make decisions relating to such matters as career, if progress is to be made into adulthood.

From the interaction of these two processes he postulated the existence of four possible identity conditions, which he called Identity Statuses. The first two correspond to the obvious situations of identity achievement, in

Figure 4(a) and 4(b):   Development of Identity Statuses:
(a) as originally proposed by Marcia (1966)
(b) a variant suggested by the author, more in tune with contemporary thinking

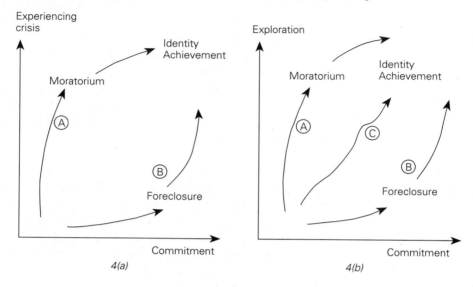

4(a)   4(b)

which the person has experienced crisis and made a commitment, and identity diffusion, in which neither process has been undertaken, (Erikson initially wrote of identity confusion, but in his later work he used the term identity diffusion). Marcia then suggested that there were also two possible intermediate positions, the states of moratorium and foreclosure. As noted earlier, Erikson had already used the word moratorium to describe a feature of contemporary society that it is often possible for a young person, particularly if undergoing higher education, to defer identity choices, and enjoy an extended adolescence. In addition, Marcia recognized that some identity decisions may be made by foreclosure, by seizing on a solution without subjecting it to personal scrutiny. He suggested that these two intermediate states represented possible resting points in the path of identity development.

The relationship between the two processes and four statuses, as originally conceived by Marcia, is demonstrated in *Figure 4(a)*. Some people will undergo a moratorium and follow route A, while others may follow the alternative route B and enter foreclosure. I propose a variant on this model, shown in *Figure 4(b)*, using the term *exploration* to replace that of *experiencing crisis*, and also show a third developmental possibility, indicated by route C, to describe those who proceed through adolescence and seemingly achieve a sense of identity without revealing any signs of real trauma.

Marcia (1966) defined the statuses thus:

> . . . an identity-achievement subject has experienced a crisis and is committed to an occupation and ideology. He has seriously considered occupational choices. With respect to ideology, he seems to have re-evaluated past beliefs and achieved a resolution. . . . (pp. 531–32)

He says that an identity diffusion person:

> Although he may mention a preferred occupation, he seems to have little conception of its daily routine . . . He is either uninterested in ideological matters or takes a smorgasbord approach. (p. 532)

He says of the moratorium subject:

> The moratorium subject is in the crisis period . . . His sometimes bewildered appearance stems from his vital concern and internal preoccupation with what occasionally appear to him to be unresolvable questions. (p. 532)

Finally, he suggests that the foreclosure subject is distinguished by:

> . . . not having yet experienced a crisis, yet expressing commitment. It is difficult to tell where his parents' goals for him leave off and where his begin. He is becoming what others prepared or intended him to become . . . (p. 532)

Some adolescents may experience the turbulence of moratorium, as shown in route A. This individual may be concerned about a whole range of issues: the purpose of life, such as the existence of God, the dangers of nuclear warfare or worldwide pollution, dealing with an emerging sense of sexuality and finding a suitable and satisfactory career. Such adolescents will display labile moods, switching from idealism to cynicism, optimism to despair, at bewildering speed. The period of moratorium is painful, both for the adolescent experiencing it and for others who are close, and that discomfort provides powerful motivation to move on, by making decisions to achieve an identity. Only a few people carry into their adult years the sense of being perpetual adolescents locked in an unending moratorium.

The second possibility is route B. Here the adolescent tries to avoid the inevitable disquiet attached to the process of self-examination involved in experiencing crisis and opts instead for ready-made solutions. Ideas are accepted from parents and peers and uncritically adopted as one's own. Unlike the moratorium subject, there is no immediate psychodynamic push for the foreclosure person to move on. The individual has reached an apparently secure position, and can remain there indefinitely. Nevertheless, it represents a false maturity, and as such can present difficult choices later on. Either one has to go back and undergo some self-examination, a delayed process of active thought and experiencing crisis in order to achieve a genuine personal identity, or one resists all challenges to the accepted beliefs and values. The foreclosure subject will often try to avoid talking about issues which challenge their brittle quasi-maturity. The possession of an authoritarian or dogmatic personality is characteristic of an individual locked into a foreclosed stance.

Marcia only postulated identity development occurring through one of these two routes. However, empirical evidence suggests that many adolescents avoid these extremes and follow route C. They will experience at intervals small areas of concern, requiring active thought, before making a commitment in that area and moving on to the next phase. For them the task of achieving a personal identity occurs fairly uneventfully.

The three possible routes shown in *Figure 4(b)* only represent the main processes and broad outcomes, clearly more detail can be added. For example, someone holding a foreclosure position is not likely to slip easily into identity achievement, as the arrow continuing route B implies, but will almost certainly have to undergo a measure of the self-questioning and uncertainty, characteristic of the moratorium position, before achieving a mature identity.

Two key questions, those of regression and decalage, are not directly tackled in Marcia's model, although later work has shed light on these issues. If someone displays identity achievement at some stage of their life then can they regress to one of the less mature statuses, without being judged as clinically abnormal? Waterman (1982) describes all the possible pathways for change between statuses and clearly sees all being perfectly viable options. It can be argued that different phases of life present different challenges and the individual has to change to cope with these. In a world of rapid social change personal identity is not necessarily fixed for the lifetime at adolescence but has to be reconsidered and renegotiated at intervals, and in this process some apparent regression may occur. It might be noted that although in everyday usage the word 'regression' might suggest something undesirable, psychologists recognize that it may represent a necessary intermediate step in achieving a more satisfactory state.

The second question, that of decalage, can be framed as follows: will an individual show the same identity status in all aspects of their life? Can someone who has achieved identity in relation to their career, for example, show a less mature status with respect to their sexuality or ideology? This simple question generates a complicated reply. On one hand people usually display some consistency, so that on balance someone less mature on one measure will probably be so on others. Nevertheless, there is not complete uniformity and again we recall the Coleman focal model. We cannot, therefore, infer with certainty anything about identity development in one area by evidence gained about another.

Marcia's four identity statuses model had an immediate appeal. It corresponded to the clinical experience of many psychologists and also made links possible between identity development and other areas of psychology.

His model also has implications for research methodology. For example, it is relatively easy to construct a questionnaire which establishes whether a subject has made firm commitments about various aspects of life. However, it is not easy to design a simple questionnaire which establishes whether the process of active thought, of exploration, has been undergone in making these commitments. In other words, questionnaires will not readily distinguish between identity achievers and foreclosure subjects, both of whom express firm commitments. Likewise, it is difficult to distinguish the indecision of the moratorium subject, who is trying hard to sort things out, and the identity diffusion subject, who is not making such an effort. It is for these reasons that the pencil-and-paper tests which were originally developed to test identity formation have in general proved so unsatisfactory.

Marcia overcame the problem by using semi-structured interviews to place people with respect to their identity status and most researchers have followed this precedent. Interviews allow one to find out not only what people believe, but how firm that belief is, and how the belief was reached. One obvious drawback to interviews is that they are time-consuming and make research with a large number of subjects very difficult and costly. A second limitation to Marcia's work is that he has been concerned mainly with the process of identity formation, and not with content. He has not attempted to make a taxonomy of possible responses in terms of the content of beliefs to parallel his description of how beliefs are reached.

A further limitation of Marcia's studies is that he initially only dealt with two of the three main areas, vocational identity and ideological identity, which Erikson identified as being important in identity development. Two possibilities suggest themselves for his avoidance of studying sexuality. One frequent criticism of Freud, and of many of the psychoanalysts who followed him, is that they were too concerned with sexuality, to the neglect of other important concerns. In that sense Marcia's contribution can be seen to redress the balance. A second, purely pragmatic point, relates to the actual empirical investigations. Often university students are used as the subjects, because they are readily at hand, and we can appreciate the difficulty of such students being asked details about their sexuality by staff and research students within the same university. Good clinical practice dictates that such sensitive enquiries should only be conducted by a stranger so as to minimise the fear that today's confessions are tomorrow's gossip.

More recently Marcia has been involved in research which has extended his model into two additional areas, 'attitudes towards sexual expression' and 'sex-role beliefs' (Rogow, Marcia and Slugoski, 1983).

Despite these limitations there has been no doubt that Marcia's model, and to a large extent his methodology, has dominated the research literature on personal identity since about 1970, and many references will be made to his identity statuses in later chapters in this book.

The Psychological Context

Further understanding of the identity concept can be gained by exploring its psychological context, seeing how the concept evolved and therefore the relationship with other psychological variables.

Erikson started from his knowledge of Freud's work and unlike many other disciples of Freud, such as Adler, Jung and Reich, he maintained a warm regard for his mentor, possibly because the age difference was so great that they could scarcely be seen as rivals.

It is essential in considering Freud to remember how much his ideas developed and changed in his career. Initially, he was seen to be almost entirely concerned with the functioning of the unconscious mind, but later, partly through his experience of working with soldiers suffering from stress in the 1914–18 war, he paid more attention to the ego, the more conscious part of the mind. It was at that time he proposed the threefold structure of the id, ego and super-ego (Freud, 1923).

The relationship between these three parts was dominating psychoanalytical thinking when Erikson met Freud. Erikson (1985) wrote: 'I must go back to the time of my training in Vienna — the period of ascendancy of ego psychology . . . to a young worker, the overall theory seemed to be working toward and yet stopping short of a systematic attention to the ego's role in the relationship of *individuality* and *community*' (pp. 15–16). Freud (1923) had described the ego as a 'frontier creature' which 'owes service to three masters and is consequently menaced by three dangers: from the external world, from the libido of the id, and from the severity of the super-ego'.

In essence Freud was arguing that the ego was both a frontier between parts of the individual mind and also between the individual and the outside world. Despite this claim, the subsequent attention of both Sigmund and Anna Freud was concentrated on the intrapersonal processes, partly because Freud always feared that humans tended to romanticize themselves and would neglect the dark side of themselves, represented by the id, unless constantly reminded of its importance.

Erikson saw the neglect of the frontier between self and the outside world as needing remedy and that he came to develop his notions of psychosocial development, in place of Freud's psychosexual model. He placed an increased emphasis on the conscious mind. Identity is about choice, and although unconscious processes may influence choices, it is within the conscious mind that a resolution of an identity crisis has to be made.

In dealing with the programmatic element of identity, the provision of a blueprint for future living, there is a closer link with Adler than Freud. Adler argued that behaviour is often more influenced by our anticipation of the future than our experience of the past. In his terms, we create 'a guiding fiction' for ourselves, a story about ourselves by which we live. It might be noted that this story is only fiction in the sense that it is invented, it need not be untrue. Indeed, the requirements of a satisfactory sense of identity is that it should be realistic and achieveable, and to that extent can be made true.

Another difference is that Freud had a dynamic model of the mind in which there is a struggle, a dialectic, between competing forces. The fundamental instincts of the id are seen to be opposed by the internalized social conscience of the super-ego, and this conflict is on-going. In contrast, the stage model of Erikson suggests that the uncertainty over identity can lead to a resolution in which conflict disappears, a description which is at variance with most contemporary psychology which sees an ongoing dialectic as the mainspring of thinking and learning. Perhaps it was this belief which caused

Erikson to concentrate on the content of identity resolution, rather than the process, while later workers, in particular Marcia, brought attention back to the process.

If the concept of identity statuses is valid then we would anticipate some correlation between them and other established psychological measures. Bourne (1978) and Marcia (1980) contain the most comprehensive surveys of such connections, which can be briefly summarized as follows.

There seems to be no connection between identity status and cognitive measures, such as intelligence. We would not anticipate such a link, but its absence confirms the belief that in dealing with identity development we are not looking simply at a growing intellect.

They report links with cognitive style and cognitive complexity. Foreclosure and identity diffusion subjects reveal a more impulsive way of thinking, while moratorium subjects and identity achievers are more reflective. Foreclosure people are the most authoritarian. Identity achievers and foreclosures are more field-independent, in other words, they focus on the precise task, while diffusion and moratorium subjects are more field-dependent, they are influenced more by the context. Foreclosure subjects reveal cognitively simple ideas, moratorium and achievers are more complex, while diffusion subjects reveal a confused and contradictory pattern of thought.

Finally, there are personality correlates. Moratorium subjects, not surprisingly, possess the highest degrees of anxiety. Identity achievers and moratorium subjects have the highest self-esteem.

Concern has been expressed, for example, by Cote and Levine (1983), by the failure to confirm the common assumption that Marcia's statuses should lie in a sequence: diffusion — foreclosure — moratorium — identity achievement. The findings on impulsivity/reflectivity and self-esteem are consistent with this sequence, while that on field dependence/independence is not. Possibly it is a mistake to attempt to place foreclosure and moratorium subjects in different places within a sequence. All the data suggests that diffusion subjects are the least mature and achievers are the most mature, and to that extent Marcia's model is vindicated. The ambiguity exists with respect to the intermediate statuses. Marcia's original model suggests that these two intermediate statuses each possesses one of the two characteristics of identity achievement, therefore it would be reasonable to assume either intermediate status can show up as superior to the other. This argument reinforces the point that there are different, and equally valid, routes to identity achievement, and we should not impose a hierarchy on the intermediate statuses. A study of 130 college women by Van Wicklin (1984) suggests that the dimension which separates achievers and foreclosures from the others, in other words a sense of commitment, account for 68 per cent of the variance in the population. The factor which separates achievers and moratorium subjects from the others, that of crisis or exploration, accounts for 26 per cent of the variance. It is not clear whether these figures would hold true for other populations.

Criticisms of the Identity Concept

Criticisms can be encountered at various levels, ranging from broadly based attacks on psychology *per se*, through to the allegation of specific deficiencies in the work of Erikson and Marcia.

I have adopted what some might see as an unfashionable approach in using the concept of personal identity as a central theme in this book. Post-modernists have criticized the use of overarching 'big ideas', such as Marxism and psychoanalysis, in favour of descriptions of the unique and local. It can be argued that psychological descriptions, such as those of identity, do not correspond to any tangible, demonstrable entity, and are merely convenient social constructs. These criticisms can be valuable in forcing us to constantly be aware of the danger of using concepts without recognizing their limitations. Sometimes, though, the arguments are pushed to an extreme position. In relation to identity, the extreme argument is to deny the existence of such an entity as the self, what Sampson (1989) called 'the deconstruction of self'. Individuals are seen simply as the point at which various social forces coincide, and have no more reality than the notion of a centre of gravity of an object, a hypothetical point through which the weight of the object can be seen to be centred. These arguments ignore the biological integrity of the individual, who has a physical life from birth to death and has a unique set of experiences meanwhile. They also deny the significance of such qualities as personal reflectivity and the exercise of personal responsibility. We need to go back to Descartes' dictum '*cogito ergo sum*' to see the limits of this extreme position. It is the specific criticisms of identity theory which merit attention.

Most criticisms of Erikson can be reduced to two questions: is it true that we have a fixed identity for life and is it true that the notion of identity is applicable to all?

As already hinted at in this chapter that although Erikson never specifically denied the possibility of some change after adolescence he assumed that once an identity had been achieved it would remain fairly constant. If this assumption was ever valid, and we might wonder about that, it has become increasingly difficult to justify. One dominant feature of contemporary life is that of rapid change, seen on a wide scale in technological developments and the associated social effects, and on a personal scale in the increasing rate of marriage breakdowns and redundancies in employment. Essentially, Erikson saw society as being relatively static and what an adolescent had to do was identify an appropriate niche in it. By comparison the task for the adolescent today is to find a way of joining something which itself is changing. The analogy is closer to that of attempting to catch a moving bus. In recognizing changed conception two consequences follow. At a theoretical level we have to think less about identity as a structure and more as a dynamic, evolving entity. On the practical level it does lend some credence to the argument than adolescents today face a more difficult task in entering adulthood than their predecessors.

The second question, that of whether identity theory applies to all people in all societies, needs a longer answer. In the late nineteenth century it was still possible for a psychologist to hold the view that all human behaviour, other than for the clinically insane, resulted from deliberate and conscious choices. Humans are equipped with the power of rational thought, it would be argued, and actions and behaviours are products of such thought. Even at that time this view was not unchallenged, there were strong advocates, such as Francis Galton, of the alternative belief that all human characteristics, from genius to criminality, were simply inherited. Nevertheless, the former view was widely upheld, not least because it gave a foundation to Victorian morality with its emphasis on personal responsibility for behaviour.

By the early twentieth century the old view was no longer tenable, at least not in a simplistic form. The two influences which undermined it were the works of Freud demonstrating the importance of unconscious mental processes, and of sociologists pointing out that an individual is constrained by the expectations and opportunities allowed by society. Set against that background Erikson's work can be seen as a partial return to the earlier tradition of ego psychology, for identity development is about choice.

The ongoing criticism of Erikson is that he failed to recognize the limits to personal choice. It could be argued that although highly intelligent middle-class males in Western Society have freedom to make choices, most people in the world have no option other than coping with the daily routine of survival. For example, Mancaster (1977) wrote,

> An identity crisis may be normative at Harvard, and among such persons as George Bernard Shaw, Martin Luther, and St. Augustine. It is not so with the common man — whose persons are not so cognitively equipped and/or socially encouraged to have an identity crisis. (p. 120)

Clearly such criticism must be faced directly. Perhaps the first point to be noted is that the failure to articulate a sense of identity is not necessarily indicative of its absence. Without an identity the individual lacks a programme for taking practical actions and decisions in life, so that effective living is difficult. Commonly, people who clearly cope most effectively with daily living find it difficult to make their sense of identity explicit, yet there must exist a set of implicit, unarticulated values and beliefs to guide their actions. Perhaps Mancaster was himself trapped in the belief, which he seems to attribute to Harvard, of believing in a rhetoric rather than a reality.

Has identity theory any relevance in a society of subsistence agriculture and arranged marriages? Even in rural communities of Europe two or three hundred years ago there was a surprising degree of social mobility, as the newer micro-historians remind us. It may have been inevitable that one worked on the land but neither prosperity nor poverty were inevitable. Success depended partly on the efforts of the individual. The main limitation in such societies is that the range for positive choices was limited, and if the choices made by foreclosure proved unsatisfactory, then the only scope for expressing dissatisfaction was by adoption of a negative identity — by treating the marriage partner badly, by excessive drinking or by failing to work effectively in the prescribed occupation.

Within our own contemporary society it is clear that the range of choice is more limited within some social groups. For maximum freedom of choice one needs to be aware of possibilities, have received an appropriate education and not unduly restrained by family expectations. Interestingly, that list suggests that not only members of the lowest socio-economic classes are disadvantaged, which is scarcely surprising, but also some at the other end of the scale. Inheritance of a title and the family estates also impose expectations and constraints on choice, as one is expected to provide an heir and to ensure the continuing prosperity of the family.

Overall, we might conclude that the concept of identity is applicable within a wide range of social contexts, but that the possibilities for choice and the processes of making that choice will differ. Erikson's own writing was weakest in dealing with gender, and his model of female development, where he adopted a biological determinist stance, has been seen widely as inadequate. This topic will be pursued in Chapter 4.

Identity — Issues and Interventions

Although it was argued in Chapter 1 that the majority of adolescents cope without going through too much trauma, or storm-and-stress, an appreciable number do display anomie or alienation on occasions. It is uncertain whether these two conditions, the passive apathy of anomie, and the active resistance or hostility of alienation, represent different aspects of the same effect, or whether they arise from different causal mechanisms.

Erikson (1968) provides a more elaborate taxonomy of the failure of adolescents to resolve the identity crisis. He described four symptoms of such failure.

The first problem is an inability to enter into a psychologically intimate relationship with another. We recall that achieving such a relationship was the sixth stage of his psychosocial model, and that he had a hierarchical system in which one task had to be resolved before the next could be addressed. His argument was that someone with an uncertain sense of identity would be reluctant to enter into a close relationship, as the other might seem threatening and take control of the confused self. Furthermore, it would be difficult for others to enter into relationship with a person who was so unsure of their self. It is difficult to relate to someone who is changeable and lacks resolution. It might be noted that this element of Erikson's model has been criticized as being less applicable to females than males, and there is evidence that many females develop the capacity to enter a psychologically intimate relationship prior to having a settled identity with respect to other aspects of life.

Secondly, he suggested that adolescents may display a diffusion of time perspective. It is in adolescence that a sense of personal time, of having a finite life-span, commonly emerges. This recognition acts as a spur to develop a programme or plan to live by and meanwhile attempt to make good use of time and available opportunities. A failure to achieve this sense of self can lead to denial, as shown by the adolescent who spends much of the day in bed. Another possibility is that the adolescent has so little sense of future and cannot envisage the future adult self. Nothing is then planned for the future, immediate gratification seems sensible, and unreasonable risks may be taken (Bell and Bell, 1993). In talking about the risk of suffering from HIV/AIDS adolescents sometimes reject the notion of safe sex as they do not have a notion of themselves in five or more years time.

The third possibility is that of diffusion of resources, shown by an inability to concentrate on essential tasks and the excessive expenditure of time on something trivial, almost to the point of being obsessional.

Finally, an adolescent can develop a negative identity. In this case of alienation the adolescent might join an unorthodox or anti-social group, or adopt extremes in dress and appearance. What is happening in this situation is an attempt to demonstrate autonomy, an independence from parents and teachers, but failing to find a socially acceptable way of doing so.

Adults cannot force identity achievement on others. It is, after all, an active process undertaken within the mind of the adolescent. However, we can facilitate the process. One task is to try and maintain a dialogue with the young person. This contact serves a number of purposes. We can supply information about the world, about careers, relationships and values, which inform the making of choices. In addition adults provide role models of how life might be lived. Finally, the dialogue itself might stimulate the process of exploration necessary to avoid false maturity of foreclosure.

> **Activity**
> Attempt to recall from your own experience instances of a failure of a teenager or young adult to attain identity. What were the characteristics of this phase of life? How eventually was it resolved?

Alongside this active role, of interacting with adolescents, there is simultaneously the need to allow time for exploration and indecision, for the moratorium which Erikson deemed necessary for identity achievement.

Chapter Summary

- The description of personal identity development provided by Erikson addresses the main psychological task of adolescence, and despite criticisms remains a valuable tool to understanding, and as such is used as an ongoing theme in this book.
- Erikson saw identity resolution being particularly pertinent to career, sexuality and what he called ideology, in essence personal values.

- Marcia developed a scheme of identity statuses which describes the processes of identity development.
- The extent to which individual and social diversity modifies the concept of identity development needs to be considered further.
- It is arguable that the pace of change in contemporary society makes identity achievement more difficult for adolescents today than in the past.

Further Reading

ADAMS, G.R., GULLOTA, T.P. and MONTEMAYOR, R. (Eds) (1992) *Adolescent Identity Formation*, Newbury Park, Ca.: Sage. An advanced text.

ERIKSON, E.H. (1950) *Childhood and Society*, New York: Norton and ERIKSON, E.H. (1968) *Identity, Youth and Crisis*, New York: Norton are still worth reading. (NB. these books have been reprinted in several editions, e.g. Paladin in the UK.)

KROGER, J. (1996) Identity in Adolescence, London: Routledge. This title is a bit misleading as the book covers a variety of theoretical perspectives on adolescence, and most of these are not usually those associated with the word identity, but the book provides useful reading of well established theories.

STEVENS, R. (Ed) (1996) *Understanding the Self*, London: Sage. Like the Kroger book it surveys a range of perspectives but does a better job in dealing with contemporary thinking more adequately.

Chapter 3

The Social World of Adolescents

In the last chapter the focus was on the psychology of the individual, yet it was recognized that personal identity had to be considered within a social context. In this chapter the intention is to explore the social world of adolescents, in terms of their relationships and in the ambiguity about the status of adolescents in our society.

Relations with Adults

It was seen in *Figure 3* that at one stage issues of relationships with parents was the biggest reported problem facing boys. Some tension with adult authority figures might be expected. It is difficult for those who have been responsible for children to relinquish the protective role as the children mature and, in view of the known risks to which adolescents are exposed, there are good reasons for feeling protective. At the same time, the teenagers need to satisfy themselves that their maturity is being recognized. In addition, acceptance within the adolescent peer group is dependent on demonstrating autonomy from adults. Therefore, there is likely to be a struggle between the teenagers pressing for more rights and freedoms and adults being reluctant to concede these. This difficult process of gaining acceptance to adulthood is exacerbated in our culture by several factors.

One problem is that adults and adolescents often have misunderstandings, essentially myths, about each other. The myth held by teenagers is that adults enjoy almost total freedom. They can drive, drink alcohol, enter legal agreements and choose how they spend their time. They are seen not to have to account to others. This perception is unreal because adults are constrained by legal requirements, by practical necessities, such as earning a living, and by the need to compromise with other people to retain friendships. The totally self-indulgent person would probably be friendless and unemployable. With adolescents only seeing part of the picture they tend to press for the freedoms without recognizing the concomitant responsibilities. A typical situation is one in which a young person negotiates an agreement to be allowed complete freedom within their own bedroom and then disturbs the whole household by playing very loud music. If asked to reduce the volume of the music they will complain that this request breaks the agreement and represents gross interference with their life.

Adults also have their myths. Sometimes it is to see all teenagers as drug-ridden criminals. More commonly, it is a romanticized view of young people enjoying the best years of their lives without any worries. This perceived freedom from care is envied, as is the belief that the young have such wonderful opportunities to make what they will of their life. A commonly expressed view is of regret that the adult cannot go back and build a different life with the benefit of hindsight. Spacks (1982) traces the development of such myths about youth through the last few centuries. This envy of the young can be particularly strong with adults who are dissatisfied with the choices they made earlier in their own lives. As George Bernard Shaw said: 'Youth is a wonderful thing. What a pity to waste it on children'. Two examples illustrate this point. When teaching mature university students I often encounter great enthusiasm for the work, accompanied with deep regret that they wasted so many years of their life before discovering that higher education might be possible for them. In a counselling role I have met married men and women who now realize that their sexual orientation is primarily homosexual, but who cannot act on this knowledge without damaging their spouses and children. In these instances the adults wish that they had made different choices in adolescence.

Three further factors complicate the situation. The first point is that adolescence has increasingly become extended. Earlier puberty has caused children to mature earlier but, at the same time, social changes have delayed entry to adulthood. One such change has been the increasing proportion of young people extending their formal education beyond the school leaving age of sixteen instead of entering employment. Another factor has been the perception that life on the streets is so dangerous that adults believe that there is a need to chauffeur the young person everywhere. It is easy to demonstrate changed attitudes. At the age of seven onwards I was allowed to walk a mile each way along suburban streets in London to and from school. By the age of ten I was allowed to travel at weekends with my contemporaries, but without adult company, up to central London to visit the South Kensington museums and take boat trips on the Thames. At that time the trust of our parents was seen to be reasonable. I doubt if many competent parents today would allow comparable freedom to their young. In part this change is in perception rather than reality. Certainly, the number of abductions of children has increased in recent years but this increase has come largely from the activity of estranged parents, not from abduction by strangers.

The second factor is the increasing horizontal social stratification, that is separation by age, in our society. In Southern Europe the extended family has survived to a considerable extent, so that three generations of a family may be seen walking out together. In Britain, and even more in the United States, a peer group ethos develops which stigmatizes such behaviour by adolescents as demonstrating immaturity. Even a routine activity, such as going shopping with the parents, embarrasses the adolescent. In this situation the adolescents spend most of their leisure times with peers, going to football

Table 1:   Use of illicit drugs among British 15–16 year olds

	Boys%	Girls%
Cannabis	43.6	38.0
Glues/solvents	19.7	21.0
Ecstasy	9.2	7.3
Cocaine	2.8	2.4
Heroin	1.7	1.5

(Based on MILLER and PLANT (1996))

matches, discos or the cinema together or just sitting in each other's rooms playing music. Within the last few decades there has been a decline of membership of groups, such as the scouts, guides and youth clubs, in which adolescents are to some extent supervised by adults. This change in social behaviour has reduced the opportunities for adults and adolescents to meet together and establish understanding.

The outcome of this separation of adolescents from adults is that two distinct cultures develop, each with characteristic values and beliefs. The disagreement about the use of recreational drugs epitomizes the problem. Drug taking among the young is not totally new, but what is different is that it has shifted from an activity of a minority, often seen to be deviant, to becoming socially acceptable within the peer group. Based on a survey of over 7000 young people drawn from seventy schools in Britain, Miller and Plant (1996) reported, as shown in *Table 1*, that illegal drug use is widespread, particularly cannabis. There seems to be a social divide with adolescents commonly accepting cannabis use and adults maintaining its illegality. Adolescents may argue, with some justification, that smoking cannabis or taking Ecstasy is less socially and medically damaging than the use of alcohol or tobacco. It is alcohol, they may argue, which causes aggression and road accidents. In their view the adult defence of tobacco and alcohol use, accompanied by condemnation of recreational drugs, is at best social conservatism, and at worst outright hypocrisy. One outcome of this breakdown of communication between the two age groups is that sensible education about the real hazards of drug use is inhibited.

The third factor, which is not new but contributes to the overall problem, is that as adolescents develop they tend to experience unease in talking to adults. Part of the problem comes from what Elkind (1970) has described as decentring. Children only have a limited awareness of others, mainly seeing others in terms of their interactions with oneself, rather than in leading an independent life of their own. As the first stage of decentring an adolescent becomes more aware of others but assumes that the adolescent is the focus of attention. There will be extreme self-consciousness, in which the adolescent feels others are constantly observing and judging one's behaviour. It takes greater maturity to realize that other people will have their own set of interests and concerns and are unlikely to be particularly concerned with oneself.

Alongside this self-consciousness goes a lack of confidence in handling adult discourse. The maturation from childhood brings a wider range of interests which allows a better dialogue with adults but one needs to find the appropriate language for this purpose. For example, I have found that adolescents are rarely shocked by the concepts in talking about sexual behaviour, but are embarrassed in finding the right language, not knowing whether to use the vernacular or medical terminology. One of the roles of formal sex education is to expose the young to the appropriate discourse so that they feel able to talk to adults.

Given all these difficulties, the existence of widespread myths about each other, the battle for autonomy, the horizontal stratification, the self-consciousness and the establishment of adult discourse, we can appreciate why relationships with adults may be strained. Nevertheless, the situation is less gloomy than it might seem. In school, students may have to appear resistant in order to maintain credibility with their peers, but still listen to teachers more than is apparent. Surveys reveal that children do value the ideas of their parents and even children in residential homes, who have experience of abuse in various ways from adults, still look to their adult residential social workers for guidance.

The adolescent has to balance conflicting interests. Montemayor (1994) summarizes the situation:

> These theoretical views have given rise to two clusters of relational constructs: those emphasizing relative difference during adolescence — conflict, individuation, psychological separation, and autonomy; and those emphasizing interpersonal connectedness — trust, intimacy, closeness, relative positive effect, and communication. (p. 2)

Given the tension between these two agendas we might anticipate relationships with adults will be fragile.

Does it matter that such relationships are so fragile? An affirmative answer can be given from two perspectives. In simple practical terms, adults and adolescents have to live together in the home, school and wider society, and this reality can be made more comfortable if reasonable compromises can be negotiated. The second argument is that adolescents need to interact with adults in order to facilitate their own identity development. Adults can contribute in three ways.

As noted earlier, one need for identity development is to live in a social climate which allows a period of moratorium balanced by encouragement to move on to making self-defining decisions. The identity status of adolescents, as described by Marcia, can be linked to parental background (Bernard, 1981 and Campbell, Adams and Dobson, 1984). Teenagers from homes in which parents were perceived as being distant, indifferent and ineffective tended to be still in the identity diffusion stage. Where there existed an unusually close relationship with parents then the young person might be locked into a foreclosure, in which the beliefs, values and interests of the parents were uncritically adopted for oneself. In extreme cases the lack of any perceived rules, norms and procedures leads to the confused passivity of anomie, and a too dominant and restrictive ethos leads the previously foreclosed individual to rebel and enter into a state of hostile alienation. The need for balance is clear.

The second contribution adults can make is by providing resources for making identity choices. Essentially these give the adolescent information about the world and self. Career guidance is an obvious example, in which possibilities are presented, alongside information about the requirements and nature of each possibility. Such information can be provided directly, by talk; by example, in providing a role model; and by giving direct experience, in allowing the teenager work experience or to undertake various tasks within the school, home or community.

The third function of an adult is to stimulate the teenager to actively think about identity decisions. Essentially, there is a need for an internal dialectic to occur in the adolescent mind for the necessary mental exploration to take place. In turn that internal dialectic might be initiated by an interpersonal dialectic with an adult. Vygotsky (1962) described the role of an adult in facilitating learning, which in many respects is what identity development involves. One key idea from Vygotsky is that some notions are totally familiar to the youngster, and need no repetition, while others are yet beyond their comprehension. There exists, however, an intermediate position, what he called the Zone of Proximal Development, in which the adolescent has not quite grasped an idea, but can be helped to do so with appropriate help. The word *scaffolding* is commonly used to describe the role of the teacher in supporting learners in their mental exploration of the unknown. Similarly, adults can stimulate and support the mental exploration involved in identity development.

Relations with Peers

One consequence of the deterioration of relationships with adults is a compensatory dependence on the peer group. Members of the group are likely to be undergoing similar experiences, such as the search for autonomy and dealing with emerging sexuality, so comfort can be found in being with those who share the concerns and anxieties. In early adolescence, immediately after puberty, same-sex groups dominate. Affiliation to these groups is so important than one theorist, Kegan (1982), suggests that there is a distinct stage in psychosocial development between latency and the search for identity. He identifies the psychosocial task or crisis resolution, to use Erikson's term, as being as achieving affiliation and avoiding a sense of abandonment. In this phase of life peer relationships are marked by 'highly invested mutuality'. Later in adolescence the group expands to include boys and girls and then fragments as the teenagers pair off in couples. It is only in these later stages that the adolescent is sufficiently confident of his or her individuality for a sense of personal identity achievement to emerge.

As a result of this closeness and sense of group loyalty young adolescents tend to be very conformist. Members of a group wear similar clothes, enjoy the same music and support the same football clubs. The image of youth as independent pioneering spirits has litle relevance at this stage. The coherence of the group is maintained by criticism or exclusion of those who do not conform. Under these conditions many adolescents will foreclose on their decisions and accept the group norms as their own. In some respects this can be a rewarding phase as close friendships are set up, but it does carry dangers. Group dynamics can be such that people behave differently within a group than they would do individually. The temptation to attract respect for being daring, and the fear of ridicule for being a 'wimp', can drive youngsters into high risk activities, which on their own they would not consider. Adding to this willingness to take risks is the fact that adolescents commonly have a distorted sense of time, feeling that life has already offered much of what is worth experiencing, and they have no wish to live for more than another few years.

This risk taking is a subject of considerable study (e.g. Bell and Bell, 1993) and is revealed in a variety of contexts. One manifestation is the reluctance of boys to use condoms despite knowing about the risk from HIV/Aids. The high crime rates of later adolescence have already been noted. Many of these criminal offences, such as stealing a car to race in a joy-ride around the neighbourhood, come not from financial necessity but more from a sense of challenge and danger. Particularly among boys there is a respect for someone who is seen to be 'cool' or 'hard'. This ethos demands a willingness to fight members of another group or gang should confrontation occur. Among girls the pressure to conform is just as real but punishment for deviance may be more subtle.

Social pressure not only causes individuals to conform to group norms but additionally to prescribed roles within a group. Once someone has a recognized role then the expectation is that they will live up to it. One common example within a school context is the teenager who has acquired the reputation of being a wit, someone who is able to score verbal points off others. The class expectation is that this person will be cheeky to teachers. The pressure is such that the joker may persist in this role despite realizing that there is an impending risk of punishment from the teacher. Many of these roles in school are less confrontational, but still recognizable in the positioning and behaviour of the class members. In the front row are the acknowledged swots, who proclaim their interest and ability in academic work. Behind them sit the closet-swots who are also interested, but wish to appear cool. At the sides of the classroom sit those who offer an implicit contract to the teacher, that each leaves the other alone.

Within the peer group itself a variety of roles are available and Youniss, McClellan and Strouse (1994) provide a six-fold taxonomy gained from a study of 905 American youths. Their categories were:

- Populars — those who enjoyed good looks, sociability and being seen to be cool;
- Jocks — essentially those with sports orientated interests;
- Brains — those recognized as being academically able;
- Normals — average, socially joining in;
- Loners — felt, and seen to be alone, nonconformist;
- Druggies/Toughs — demonstrably anti-social, aggressive, overtly using drugs.

It is not clear whether the same principal categories would emerge within other cultures. Observation of British adolescents suggests that the status of these sub-group members would shift with maturation. In early adolescence academic interests and achievement do not confer high status, but maturation and the approach of the GCSE examinations at the age of sixteen often leads to these qualities becoming more valued. Similarly, nonconformity from the group ethos tends be tolerated more among older adolescents than those younger.

Although there are negative aspects to peer influences these should be balanced against two major positive effects. The first is the recognition that it is among their peers that adolescents are likely to find their spouse, their friends and their work colleagues, and learning to work with these people is essential to successful living in adulthood. Group activities provide a forum for developing social skills and understanding of others.

The second important factor is that peer relationships contribute to the social construction of identity. Remembering Erikson's phrase that identity is about 'samenesses and differences' then the arena of the close knit peer group provides an opportunity for the individual to locate oneself. It is in comparision with others of similar age and background that adolescents gain a sense of their individual qualities.

Sub-cultures and Gangs

Young people are likely to identify with those most similar to themselves, drawn from the same locality and of similar social class. An adolescent in a deprived inner city area may not have much in common with someone living in a prosperous suburb. Hence, identification is less with the total adolescent population of the country and more with sub-cultures within it. Recognition of this reality has led to a number of classic studies of specific sub-cultures, e.g. Willmott (1969) of boys in East London and Coffield, Borrill and Marshall (1986) of three groups of young people in the North East of England.

Sub-groups differ in their social origins and also in their allegiances to football teams and music groups. These variables are intertwined in various ways. For example, whether someone in Glasgow supports Rangers or Celtic football teams is as much an expression of background as current choice. The former team draws most of its support from Protestants and Celtic from Roman Catholics, a division which echoes the situation in Ulster.

The rivalry in the early 1960s between Mods and Rockers epitomizes many of the characteristics of adolescent sub-cultures. Both groups asserted independence from the adult culture of the time, but did so in different ways. The Rockers social cohesion was built around the use of powerful motor bikes, with the concomitant dress in leather. Their appearance, with long, untidy hair, seemed to be an overt assertion of rebellion from adult norms. They were the teenagers which adults might dread. The Mods adopted a neat appearance with well-tailored clothes and carefully cut hair. At first sight they appeared to be more conforming with adults, until it is realized that they were modelled on American East Coast style. They asserted their difference from adults in a more subtle way. At a time when many men had a short back and sides haircut the carefully layer cut of the young Mods was an expression of difference, of being more sophisticated and cosmopolitan than their parents. To the Mods the Rockers appeared crude and unwashed. To the Rockers the Mods appeared effete. Thus, each sub-group was able to define itself as being different from each other as well as being different from adult society. Each group had carefully defined characteristics allowing members to recognize a kindred spirit.

In communities where there is widespread unemployment and crime then the defining characteristics of a sub-group may be largely negative, expressed in non-conformity and challenge to others. The extreme end of this process is to have gangs consisting largely of those who have become alienated from conventional society, such as those 'bunking off' from school and those excluded from school. The roots of delinquency are complex, being in part learned behaviour, so that adult role models may make a causal contribution. However, increasingly it has become the belief that membership of a particular peer group is crucial. Coleman and Hendry (1990) sum up the evidence:

> Delinquents tend to live in close proximity to one another . . . Spontaneous comments from youths suggests that disengagement from the influence of peer groups was an important feature in the abandonment of delinquent habits. (p. 133)

Under these conditions adults face a tricky situation if they suspect that a teenager is being drawn into crime or delinquent behaviour by peers. Direct confrontation may be counter productive and the better tactic may be by indirect means, by changing routines and practices in some way so that the adolescent has an opportunity for redefinition.

The Loner

It has long been traditional in teacher training to point out that most teachers pay attention to noisy and disruptive pupils, for very obvious reasons, but ignore someone who is quiet and withdrawn, who may be in greater need for help. Adolescence is a time when certain adult mental disorders, such as schizophrenia, tend to be first manifest, so there is some basis for concern. Wolff (1993) surveys the possibilities of personality difficulties becoming evident in this way. However, we may now be falling into the danger of seeing all detachment as being unhealthy. Dowrick (1992) argues about the need for balance:

> Each of us needs to find a delicate, shifting balance between dependence and independence, between being open to others and taking care of ourselves. Each of us have our own needs for solitude and intimacy. (p. xxii)

The adolescent who is something of a loner may be unhappy but equally may simply be self-sufficient. Extroverts not only enjoy a full social life but require it. Left to their own devices they are likely to become bored and depressed. A more introverted person needs less external stimulus and is more able to enjoy Wordsworth's 'bliss of solitude'. One advantage of having some time on their own is that it gives the adolescent space to undertake the mental exploration of possibilities necessary for identity development. A life of frenetic social activities, where the television is always playing when one is alone, may inhibit this identity formation process. It is reasonable to be concerned if we see a young person as being rather withdrawn, but attempt to distinguish this situation from that of happy self-containment.

Fortunately, schizoid behaviour is relatively rare and adolescent loneliness more often is symptomatic of a temporary developmental phase. The young person who is maturing at a different rate from most of the peers may be out of step with the others. A slow maturer may find it difficult to adjust to the new interests and life style demanded by the group. An early developer might find peers to be too childish. There can be a loss of confidence, for example someone who has a physical defect may become more conscious of it in adolescence when worries about being sexually attractive emerge. These problems, combined with the feeling of being 'in between', neither child nor adult, may cause adolescents to withdraw for a time and spend time on solitary pursuits, such as fishing or playing with the computer. Only if this tendency is extreme and prolonged is there cause for concern.

The Status of the Peer Group

Our working with adolescents is confused by a variety of ambiguities and contradictions. One boy commented to me, 'Half the time adults tell me that

I am too young to do something, the rest of the time they are telling me to grow up'. This statement captures the uncertainty we have about adolescence. In many respects children in the past have been seen as miniature adults, and prior to the Factory Acts in Britain in the first half of the nineteenth century, it was thought appropriate that they should work long hours in factories. With respect to adolescence there was an obvious class difference with those from wealthier homes, particularly the boys, enjoying the moratorium of an extended education, while others were apprenticed at an early age into adult employment. The raising of the school leaving age to sixteen and the lack of employment for unskilled youth has transformed the situation, but ambiguity remains. Simultaneously, the teenagers are now both marginalized and privileged.

They are marginalized in a variety of ways. These include legal constraints, of not being able to join the electorate or enter into legal contracts until the age of eighteen. In practice, the labour market tends to marginalize them as employers often look for some track record of diligent and successful working in taking on new recruits. In this situation they cannot gain the necessary experience to attract employers, and without employment they are not financially independent, so become marginalized within much of the economy.

At the same time there has been the counter trend of a niche market developing within the economy targeted on teenagers. It is difficult to locate with certainty when this trend first started, but I think it was in the 1950s, with the growth of rock-and-roll music, possibly the first genre of music aimed at adolescents rather than adults. Certainly, since that time there has been an explosive growth of activity in retailing music and clothes for the young. It has now become a widely accepted belief that the young should have the resources to participate in these elements of the peer culture. In this sense adolescents have become a privileged group.

At this point, we encounter a further twist in the story: that adolescents are often exploited by adults. Both the clothes and music industries are dominated by the notion of contemporary fashion, the necessity of being up-to-date in one's possessions. The consequence of this manipulation of the market is a rapid turnover, as yesterday's music and clothes are abandoned long before reaching the end of their useful life. The essence of pop charts for music is to see what is in favour this week. Football clubs have exploited the same demand of being 'with it' by frequently changing the strip, the colours of the players clothes, so fans have to buy another set of matching items to demonstrate their support to the club.

Perhaps the extreme example of exploitation is with respect to drugs and prostitution. On one hand, we have legions of adults, parents, teachers, doctors and social workers, attempting to steer the young away from drug use and addiction. At the same time, we have another cohort of adults, fewer in number but individually wealthier, making their living by supplying drugs. If the individual adolescent cannot afford to maintain their drug habit then another friendly adult will be willing to suggest quick ways of earning money, notably through prostitution.

There is uncertainty of what we should expect from our adolescents, their role, rights and responsibilities. Through marketing we raise their expectations, but through changes in the labour market we make it extremely difficult to realize these expectations. This contradiction, combined with effects, such as the increased horizontal stratification already discussed, makes the passage into adulthood that much more problematic.

One of the first persons to detect the problem was Friedenberg (1959) who argued that the essential task of adolescence, that of using the moratorium to explore identity options, had to be a personal endeavour. Individuals need to be detached from the conformist pressures of childhood and adulthood for a while to enter a degree of solitude in order to allow themselves space to undertake this exploration. Friedenberg then argued that the existence of the commercially driven conformist youth culture took away the opportunity for individuals to explore possibilities on their own. Furthermore, the visible lifestyle of youth provided a target on whom adults could project their own anxieties: 'I do believe that the hostility towards the adolescent is one more index of the rootlessness of modern life' (p. 131).

Social Identity

As indicated earlier, this term describes a range of phenomena. Sometimes it relates to a collective sense of identity, that which is commonly expressed by a social sub-group, for example a particular set of immigrants. The alternative interpretation is to see how membership and non-membership of certain social groups impacts on the personal sense of identity possessed by individuals. It is this latter sense that the notion of social identity is being pursued here.

It has already been argued that people gain a sense of identity through comparisons with other people within a group. The foundation of social identity theory by Tajfel (e.g. 1978) is that identity is also gained by making comparisons between groups. People will identify with their own class, race, gender, or similar social variable, and see how members of this group are positioned in society. Social identity develops from an internalization of the images, albeit stereotyped, of the groups to which one does and does not belong.

At its simplest this notion can slip into a social determinist theory; that a person is solely defined by group membership. The arguments against this position, as against biological determinism, is that the person is not credited with the capacity to reflect and make choices. Personal responsibility is denied. However, much of the work in the field (e.g. Breakwell, 1986 and Hogg and Abrams, 1988) recognize the interaction between social positioning and a personal sense of identity.

One traditional example might be of a young person being brought up within a working-class family and community, in which no one had gone into higher education, who then gains a place at university. What effect does moving away from home and living in a community which is dominated by middle-class mores have on the individual? Does the student attempt social mobility by copying the speech and behaviour of the new peers or is the sense of personal roots strengthened? The outcome to this dilemma will depend on such variables as the degree of stress within the prevailing situation, the ambitions of the individual, and their resources in knowing how to and being able to change. Shaw's story, *Pygmalion*, is that of someone acquiring some of the resources to move between social classes, but gaining acceptance within another ethnic group may be less easy.

Questions such as these raise issues of salience of group membership. There was a famous encounter at a women's meeting in the United States when one speaker said 'When we look into a mirror all of us in this room see a woman . . .' to be interrupted by someone saying, 'When I look into a mirror I see a *black* woman'. Not only will salience vary between members of the same groups but also vary for an individual according to the context. Many of us may not be overtly conscious of our gender within much of our daily life, but when finding oneself the sole person of this gender within a group its salience will be highlighted.

The significance of the notions of social identity to adolescence is that young people are likely to go through a number of changes in group membership and identification. From being defined as a child, living within the social ambit defined by school and home, they enter the somewhat confused position of being a teenager. Then, shortly afterwards, they may have to undergo a further set of redefinitions on leaving home and entering higher education or employment. The advantage of social identity theory is that it does spell out the change mechanisms involved in these processes.

Chapter Summary

- Relations between adults and adolescents are liable to be strained as issues of autonomy and responsibility emerge, misunderstanding and myths about each other exacerbate the tensions;
- The psychological development of the adolescent can, for example, in decentring, contribute to the problem;
- Adolescents compensate for the separation from adults by entering close-knit peer groups bound by shared interests and values, these peer groups provide valued friendships but also can enhance what adults see as anti-social behaviour;
- The ambivalent role of adolescents in society generates confusion;
- The study of social identity provides a tool for analysing aspects of adolescent development.

Further Reading

COTTERELL, J. (1966) *Social Networks and Social Influences in Adolescence*, London: Routledge. Much of the evidence relates to Australia, but the issues are similar.

DAVIS, J. (1990) *Youth and the Condition of Britain: Images of Adolescent Conflict*, London: The Athlone Press. A good review with interesting material from recent history.

DEAUX, K. (1991) 'Social identities; thoughts on structure and change', in Curtis, R.C. (Ed) *The Relational Self: Theoretical Convergences in Psychoanalysis and Social Psychology*, New York: Guilford. Deaux, of all the social identity theorists, has made the most connections with Eriksonian ego identity.

HOGG, M.A. and ABRAMS, D. (1988) *Social Identifications: A Social Psychology of Intergroup Relations and Group Processes*, London: Routledge. A British source and provides a good introduction to the field.

Chapter 4

Diversity Among Adolescents: The Case of Gender

In Chapter 2 the question of the applicability of Erikson's ideas of identity to all adolescents, regardless of gender and social context, was discussed. How significant are these differences on identity development? One writer, Kiell (1967) had no doubts, asserting: 'It is my thesis that the great internal turmoil and external disorder of adolescence are universal and only moderately affected by cultural determinants' (p. 9). He gathered a range of accounts, going back to the times of Classical Greece, to illustrate consistent themes, such as sexual awakening, the first love, peer culture, the influence of charismatic teachers and intellectual development.

It is difficult to do justice to both the commonality and diversity, as many aspects have been inadequately researched and theorized. Part of the diversity comes from individual idiosyncrasies and it is difficult to generalize about these. Of the social variables of gender, class and race only the former has been well described, principally through the powerful influence of feminism in recent decades. In many instances it is difficult to disentangle race from social class, so observed differences can be interpreted in different ways. With gender we find it easier to compare like with like, that is boys with girls from the otherwise similar backgrounds, but even here interactions complicate the picture. It seems that in the contemporary British culture boys of Afro-Caribbean origins and girls from Islamic homes experience particular difficulties, with the gender and race interaction producing outcomes more than the sum of the individual separate factors. To simplify the situation I am taking gender as the main tool for analysis.

The military historian Corelli Barnett has used the title *The Audit of War* (Barnett, 1986) to describe the strength of nations. His thesis is that prior to a war national leaders can engage in extensive rhetoric about the power of their country, but when at war a conclusive audit takes place, as it emerges for which countries the rhetoric matches reality. I see a description of gender differences both being important in its own right and also providing an audit of our thinking. If a psychological theory does not adequately describe both men and women then clearly it is at fault.

Gender and Psychology

It is ironic that within psychology, which attracts an unusually high proportion of females to its workforce, we find many extreme examples of male bias and dominance. Many studies made by male psychologists of male populations have been generalized so that the findings are to be applied to all people. Take, for example, the opening words of a report on male adolescents, 'Like its predecessor *Contrary Imaginations*, this book deals with differences in human intellect — differences, that is, in the ways in which people think, in the frames of mind they characteristically adopt' (Hudson, 1968). The evidence from males is being used to generalize about all people and the possibility that there may be significant gender differences is not considered.

Where females have been discussed it is often in terms of being like men, with a few specified differences. Such conceptualization immediately sets up the male situation as the norm, and the female differences can almost be seen as being deviant, or what Simone de Beauvoir (1949) described as 'the other' (see *Educating the Other* by Carrie Paechter in the same series as this book). Like Professor Higgins in *My Fair Lady*, the lament is why cannot women be more like men. This bias, which usually comes from default rather than intent, can even affect the judgment of clinical psychologists, who, one would presume, would be most alert to the danger of such bias. Broverman *et al.* (1970) made a study of seventy-nine clinically trained psychologists, of whom thirty three were women. Using a 122-item questionnaire, they were asked to identify the characteristics of a healthy, mature and socially competent male, a similar female, and a similar adult person of unspecified sex. It was found that the clinicians, regardless of their own sex, saw males and females differently, with the male ideal corresponding closely with the human (adult of unspecified sex) ideal. Similarly, there has been a recognition in recent years that in psychometrics many standard tests have a sex bias (Selkow, 1984).

Within the last two decades there has arisen a counter-culture of feminist psychology which needs to be read alongside the earlier mainstream work. For example, in Chapter 7 we shall see how Gilligan (1982a) provided such a critique of Kohlberg's work on moral development. Above all, it is Freud who has been subjected to the most scrutiny, for example by Mitchell (1975). As Freud had such a strong influence on Erikson, and hence on identity theory, we need to look at the arguments in some detail.

The first doubt might be about the uncritical biological determinism of Freud, and in the next section the limitations of such an approach will be argued. The second concern is that values are attached to biological differences. Girls are seen to experience penis envy while boys fear castration. Males possess that which is desirable, so they enjoy a superiority, while females can only envy them. The possibility of uterus envy, in which males envy the capacity of women to bear children, is not considered. A further doubt might be whether children are even aware of differences in genitalia. Unless they have seen someone of the other sex undressed they would not possess the knowledge central to Freud's model.

The value system comes out in the language employed:

We do not, of course know the biological bases of these *peculiarities* of women . . . She acknowledges the fact of her castration, and with it, too, the

> *superiority* of the male and her own *inferiority* . . . When a girl discovers her own *deficiency* . . . She clings obstinately to the expectation of one day having a genital of the same kind. (Freud, 1977, pp. 376–80, my emphasis)

Even allowing for the problem of translation from the original German, it is difficult to justify value-laden terms like inferiority and deficiency in a description of anatomical differences.

Elsewhere he wrote on the choices open to women. 'One leads to sexual inhibition or neurosis, the second to a modification of character in the sense of masculinity complex and the third to formal feminism'. He argued that only the third choice, the acceptance of a traditional feminine role leads to happiness. In contrast, he argued that the second option, which might open more choice for women comparable to the position for a man, would produce 'polymorphous perversity'. In this event, women may be seen to have little sense of identity other than waiting for the right man to arrive.

Finally, Freud can be accused of dismissing accounts from women of early childhood sexual experience as pure fantasy. Evidently, when he first heard such accounts he believed that they might be true but was later persuaded to treat them as fantasy (Masson, 1984). He then became concerned why so many women should invent such stories and this line of questioning led to the development of Oedipal theory. More recent work suggests that child abuse is not uncommon, and in that event he may have compounded the misery of the women by refusing to accept their accounts. In this matter we must attempt to keep a sense of balance. Some allegations of abuse may well be untrue, and the possibility of fantasy should be kept in mind, but the very least we can do for those who report such experiences is to take them seriously. Somewhere along the line Freud lost that sense of balance with respect to this issue.

Recalling how strongly Erikson was influenced by Freud we might anticipate a similar bias in the conceptualization of identity, and the existence of a female alternative, but before we can examine Erikson's writing on these issues we need to employ a consistent nomenclature relating to sex and gender.

Sex, Gender and Sexuality

Throughout the literature on identity we find reference to 'sex role' as being crucial. What does this term mean? Erikson, as we have already noted, stated that difficulties relating to sex role lead to 'bisexual confusion'. Clearly he was writing about sexuality. However, most later writers, still employing the term sex role, deal with the differences between men and women, in the ways identity develops and the content of identity. They are describing gender differences. To proceed any further with the analysis we need to distinguish between the words sex, gender and sexuality.

A convention about the use of these words has become widely accepted in recent years: we should only talk of sex differences to describe that which is manifestly biological in origin, notably the different genitalia, reproductive function, and the ability to suckle a child. The word gender should be used to describe differences which are not manifestly biological in origin, and may well be the product of social processes. Sexuality refers to the erotic and emotional response of an individual. If we use these rules we can then separate out a number of different ways in which identity may be involved.

We can envisage how a small minority of people might experience difficulties with sex and identity. Some people may have some ambiguity about their biological sex. In the extreme case there is the rare condition of hermaphroditism, in which a child is born with intermediate genitalia. More commonly, but still quite rare, hormonal disturbance can produce some secondary sex characteristics of the other sex. For example, a boy at puberty may experience breast enlargement. There is also the situation experienced by transsexuals, who possess perfectly normal bodies and genitalia, but who have a clear sense of identity that they should be of the other sex. They feel as if the psyche has become trapped in the wrong body. For the psychologist interested in identity formation, the issue of trans-sexuality is important and puzzling. It is fair to say that the topic has been inadequately researched and I know of no convincing explanation. By contrast, the topic of sexuality and identity has been discussed in considerable detail and this issue will be explored in a later chapter. Finally, there are the questions about gender differences and identity, which are manifest in differences in identity content and in the processes leading to identity development. These matters are central to this book.

It must be emphasized that not only are sex, gender and sexuality conceptually different but they are not correlated in practice. For example, the fact that a person displays psychological androgyny, that is possess some of the gender characteristics associated with each sex, is in no way indicative of bisexuality. Similarly, it would be erroneous to see trans-sexuality as being a variant of homosexuality, as the following comment by a young male-to-female trans-sexual might indicate.

> I lead a fairly sexless sort of life. The only person who attracts me is a man, who sees me as a woman, and wants to make love to me as a woman. Until I have the operation that is impossible. No heterosexual man would fancy me and I would not want to go with a gay man, as he would be attracted to me for the wrong reasons . . . My only real friends are a few girls, who know all about me. We go shopping together and enjoy the usual 'girls' talk' . . . Even masturbation is not enjoyable, because it reminds me of the mix-up with my body.

Although the use of this convention relating to these three terms clarifies many points it must be admitted that some issues are still open to argument. We have defined gender as relating to that which is not manifestly biological, which are presumed to come from social causes, but we cannot be certain that the absence of evidence of a direct link with biology proves that no link exists. What we have described as gender differences may, in some instances, be *indirectly* influenced by biological factors. In considering their life options adolescents can scarcely be unaware of the bodily changes which they are experiencing. The key point is that the biological influences are mediated through mental processes.

The Development of Gender Differences

Two main processes can be seen to contribute to the social development of gender prior to adolescence. The first is that of socialization. Society expects boys and girls to behave differently and social pressure tends to force people to conform to these expectations. The second influence comes from the asymmetrical experience young boys and girls have in being mothered.

The process of socialization into gender roles commences at birth. Even before a child is born the parents are likely to be talking about the possible sex of the baby. When birth occurs, alongside the news that there has been a safe delivery, the event is described in terms of the child's sex, not least because the gendered nature of language makes it difficult to talk about a child without knowing its sex. From this point onwards boys and girls will be perceived and treated differently.

Perception is more important than the actual sex of the baby. In a famous study, Smith and Lloyd (1978) observed the behaviour of young mothers who had been asked to look after another child, unknown to them, for a short time. If the women were told that the child was a boy then he was allowed freedom to move around, and restlessness was seen as indicating the need for stimulation. If the child was thought to be a girl, she was held close,. and restlessness was seen as indicating the need for comfort and reassurance. These behaviours occurred regardless of the actual biological sex of the child. These findings are most significant. It had long been known that young boys and girls tended to be treated differently, but it could be argued that the different responses from mothers arose because boys and girls were genetically coded to elicit different responses. This evidence denies the hypotheses in demonstrating that it is the *perceived* sex which is crucial.

Boys and girls are likely to be given different toys and be encouraged to play different games. By the age of two or three awareness of one's own sex is central to the developing sense of identity: children usually describe themselves in terms of their name, age and sex. By the age of two and three children have a clear sense of gender roles, believing that girls would clean the house when they had grown up, while the boys would undertake different tasks, such as mowing the lawn (Kuhn *et al.*, 1978). Many elements of school life are likely to reinforce this sense of gender differentiation. While writing this book I heard of an incident in which a naughty boy aged seven was made to sit with the girls at the other end of the room as a punishment. Even in schools which try to minimize the gender differences most groups of children playing together in the playground are likely to be composed of one sex. At the age of four years children spend three times as much time playing with same sex partners as cross-sex. By the age of six and a half years, this ratio is 11:1 (Maccoby and Jacklin, 1987). A boy or girl who persists in playing with the other sex will be subjected to considerable teasing, so there is a powerful social control ensuring the maintenance of single-sex groups. This social control is much stronger for boys. The girl who is a Tomboy may meet some criticism, but often no more than amused tolerance. The boy who is thought to be effeminate usually meets savage criticism from peers, and anxious concern from his parents, with the so-called 'feminoid' boys being judged as suffering from a disorder requiring treatment (Rekers and Yates, 1976).

After this stage each single-sex group develops its own dynamics. For example, Malz and Borker (1983) report that boys' groups will be marked by competition, and members constantly interrupt each other, and often introduce a new topic ignoring the previous speaker. Within girls' groups there will be more support for each other, with most contributions referring back to the previous speaker. When, perhaps in a classroom, boys and girls have to work together, the group dynamics may not be helpful, particularly for girls having to handle the competitive mode of boys. Particular problems arise when boys and girls have to share possessions. Charlesworth and La Freniere (1983) studied what happened when groups consisting of two boys and two girls were presented with an apparatus for viewing a film which only allowed one child to watch at a time. On average, boys spent three times as long viewing as the girls. Similar effects are reported in school classrooms (Stanworth, 1983) with girls being pushed aside in lessons involving the use of computers or apparatus.

This competitive element with boys can be legitimized by games and sports which permit physical competition and aggression within prescribed limits. In many contexts fights are only avoided by creating elaborate rules for behaviour and established hierarchies of social dominance. Often, all male groups, such as in some schools, the military, or sports clubs, are marked by the central role of ritual, of hierarchy made manifest through a dress code and the wearing of badges and insignias, and a clear definition of what constitutes acceptable behaviour. For an outsider, as women must be in this context, it is difficult to understand how the complex social system works and, inadvertently, one may transgress the unspoken rules. These implicit social norms provide a further barrier to women attempting to enter male dominated institutions, such as in business, the traditional professions such as law, and parliament.

By contrast, girls tend to be less competitive and more cooperative. Askew and Ross (1988) describe what happens if pairs of children are asked to paint a picture together. A pair of girls will discuss the task and then cooperate in its completion. A pair of boys may draw a line down the centre and then each boy will paint in his half without any regard for the other.

In this fashion children are socialized into gender roles, prepared to enter a world in which men and women are distinguished at every level, including name, dress, patterns of employment, caring for children, and social customs. Even our languages, with which we think and communicate, reflect a world divided by gender. In many languages the names of all objects are grammatically masculine or feminine. In English it is difficult to select neutral pronouns in place of he/she or him/her. Perhaps the most revealing linguistic custom is to talk of the opposite sex, remembering the word has the same root as 'oppose', rather than using a neutral term such as the 'other sex'. As a consequence of all these effects the child grows up in a world in which sex differences are seen to be important. Socialization takes place in two stages. Initially a child may conform to society's rules simply because it is easier to do so than otherwise. Later on, these societal norms can become so internalized the individual ceases to recognize that they come from the prevailing views in our culture rather than possessing some intrinsic validity.

Chodorow (1978) has drawn attention to the second main causal factor of gender differentiation, that both young boys and girls are usually cared for by a woman. The experience of early childhood is therefore asymmetrical. The girl is brought up by someone with whom she can make a complete identification, but although the boy may start relating to his mother in a similar way he is likely to be told that he must be different. In our culture the boy who is seen to be effete or girlish is likely to encounter censure. It is believed that boys should not cry. They are expected to be tough and independent. Girls can learn femininity by imitation and identification but boys have to learn masculinity by separation and censure.

Essentially, Chodorow's thesis was based on a particular development from psychoanalysis, known as object relations, a notion introduced by Klein (1932) and later developed by others, such as Winnicott (1986). The key notion within this model is that a person relates to a series of significant objects in their life. Initially this is likely to be the mother. Girls can slowly shift their attention from the mother to other objects but with boys this process is accelerated such that the boy may feel lost. He may be reluctant to trust other people and attach more significance to other objects, to toys and pets, to his computer, or even to an ideology. Chodorow argued that a cycle is created, with these early childhood experiences affecting the way boys and girls mature so that they in turn perpetuate the process by their treatment of their own offspring. Chodorow makes the distinction between bearing a child, which for biological reasons can only be done by woman, and rearing a child which is only associated with womanhood by social custom. Mothers tend to keep their daughters close to them so that the girls grow up with a strong sense of relating to others, and this quality prepares them for the child rearing role with the next generation. In fact, she argues, the widespread female wish to become a mother owes more to this social conditioning than to a biological need. Young boys are encouraged to be more independent and less free in the expression of emotion and these qualities tend to inhibit them in child rearing. Therefore, to understand the total process, we need to look at both the psychology of the individual, particularly in early childhood, and the sociology of gender, for these elements interact and reinforce each other.

Within traditional cultures this gender differentiation arising from child rearing served a social purpose. In times of war young men were sometimes asked to sacrifice their lives for the nation and their identification with abstract notions of patriotism and service caused them to do so. These notions had become the significant objects in their life. For example, in reading about the appalling slaughter in the 1914–18 war in which Britain lost over a million people, the surprise is just how little desertion or tendency to mutiny was manifested. Making motherhood the central role for women exercised another aspect of social control, not least in leaving the labour market more open to men. It might be argued that this gender distinction has less utility and is less acceptable in contemporary society.

The gender differences affect adult behaviour. Women tend to be less confident and blame themselves for any problems experienced in life, and will have a weaker sense of personal autonomy. Men will benefit from being more confident and less upset by a failure, tending to blame others or external events for problems. Men tend to be extrapunitive while women are intrapunitive. Men may be the beneficiaries in terms of autonomy, but they pay a price in at least two separate ways.

As we have seen, girls receive more talk from the mother and engage in a more meaningful dialogue with each other in conversation, and from this experience are likely to develop a greater sense of empathy for others. Adolescent boys are often exploitive, seeing parents as a source of money, and judging girls solely in terms of their willingness to engage in sexual activities with them (Lees, 1987). Whereas girls recognize the potential for developing a more equal and reciprocal relationship with parents, and they are more likely to judge others, including boys, in wider terms than their sexual appeal. The consequence of these social differences is that women are likely to be more sensitive in handling social relationships, and more willing to work together cooperatively.

The second penalty experienced by men comes from their emotional reticence, which provides a brittle quality, a surface hardness accompanied by severe damage if this surface is fractured. Lynn (1962) argued that men are often insecure as they experienced too early and abrupt a separation from their mother. A close relationship with the father can help at this stage, but often the father plays a smaller part in child care, so that the boy experiences isolation and an unwillingness to trust others. Expression of emotions, as any psychotherapist will testify, provides the first step in understanding, management and control. The failure to admit to emotions and discuss feelings, may provide a temporary refuge, but it leaves the male vulnerable if he is forced by circumstances to enter a situation which demands emotional explicitness. For example, relationships within a family require a measure of emotional honesty and expression, and often this demand is met almost entirely by the mother and is evaded by the father. This argument demonstrates a central difference between object relations theory and Freudian ideas. To Freud men not only enjoyed in many instances economic and social advantages but were also psychologically stronger, as references to penis envy indicate. From the perspective of object relations theory although men may more commonly occupy important and well-paid posts they pay a price by being in many respects more psychologically vulnerable than women.

We should therefore recognize that both men and women pay a price for being too tightly locked into traditional gender roles. The loss for women may be more obvious, as it is manifest in such obvious things as career development, but with the less visible qualities involving emotional expression, men may experience a greater loss.

Misunderstanding can arise from the gender differences in expressing emotions. It is a common complaint of women that they feel 'shut out' by their male partners, because the men will not reveal their feelings. It is an equally common complaint of men that they feel 'shut in' by their female partners, because the women always want to know what you are feeling and will not allow you any emotional privacy and autonomy. The particularly sad feature of this situation is that it can cause a rapid deterioration in the relationship, as the expression of need by each partner can produce further resentment in the other, so the mismatch becomes an increasing source of friction.

This account of the social causation of gender differentiation relates the processes in the different experience boys and girls have in early childhood, to the outcomes, manifest in adolescence and adulthood. Therefore, unlike models of biological determinism, it is totally coherent. For this reason there has been a growing belief that observed gender differences largely develop through social processes, and gender itself is essentially a social construct.

Possibly the main weakness in the social argument is that it fails to account for the fact that in the vast majority of societies, with all their diversity of belief and custom, gender roles tend to behave much in common. Males usually carry out

> **Activities**
> Try to recall your earliest childhood memories in which you became aware of gender differences and of your own gender. If possible, share these recollections with others, perhaps initially of the same sex as yourself and then with those of the other sex. What commonality is there between the memories? Do any differences emerge in the recall of men and women?
>
> If you have access to children, either as a parent or teacher, observe the extent to which their play and choice of friends is gendered. What differences are there between the group dynamics of a group of boys and one of girls?

much of the work outside the home while women assume most responsibility in the home, including child-care. In undeveloped economies, where the work away from the home required the brute force of muscle-power, and where women faced an annual series of pregnancies, a division of labour based on biological determinants made sense. What we witness in our contemporary technological society is the existence of social mores and customs which reflect the needs of an earlier society. What was originally a sensible recognition of biological realities has become codified into a social system applying unnecessary constraints on the population. As the development of a society involves effective adaptation to changing circumstances, it can be argued that reducing the pressure to conform to gender stereotypes not only conveys greater happiness to individuals in dealing with psychological androgyny, as will be argued later in this chapter, but also produces a more flexible and dynamic society.

Psychological Androgyny

Sometimes, when I am discussing with students various research methodologies such as the use of surveys, I will ask them to work in small groups and invent some items for a questionnaire on masculinity/femininity. At this stage they do not receive any further clarification of the task. They usually start confidently, inventing items with a forced choice between options perceived to be characteristic of the two qualities. To take a rather trivial and stereotypical item they might suggest: 'Which do you prefer to watch on television, football or a cookery programme?'. After each group has invented a few such items a note of dissent usually arises and eventually they can proceed no further. The problem is that some individuals find that they cannot easily respond, as they either like both or like neither of the alternatives. In this event, they will ask should they uncouple the alternatives and ask about them separately? They have reached the purpose of the exercise, that one needs to have a clear sense of the constructs being measured before attempting to develop a test for them.

This anecdote mirrors a change in psychological thinking about gender. For a long time the implicit assumption had been that masculinity and femininity were at opposite ends of a bi-polar scale. Then, the alternative conceptualization was suggested, notably by Bem (1974 and 1975), that these qualities should be seen to lie on two independent scales. In this event we can envisage an individual gaining low or high scores on each scale, giving a total of four possible combinations. A person may gain a 'conventional' score with a high score on the characteristic associated with their sex and a low score on the other scale. It would be possible, although uncommon, for someone to have the reversed score, a trans-sex pattern. Some people will score lowly on both scales, they are said to be undifferentiated, a sign, perhaps, of immaturity. The fourth possibility, and the one which has attracted the most attention, is gaining high scores of both scales. This pattern is described as that of psychological androgyny.

The principal concern has been to determine whether androgynous individuals are disadvantaged or not. The evidence has been overwhelming, that the reverse is more commonly true, and androgyny conveys advantages of flexibility and ease of adjustment. For example, in a study of 225 high school students, Avery (1982) found that the androgynous were significantly less lonely than others, while Lamke (1992) in a survey of 106 high school students showed an association between androgyny and high levels of self-esteem. Bem, herself, saw androgynous individuals possessing the male quality of independence with the female quality of being able to express emotions openly. These findings have had a considerable influence on educational and therapy programmes. Previously, there was a widespread belief that men should be men, that women should be totally feminine, and any departure from these norms should be suppressed.

Given this evidence about psychological androgyny we need not feel worried that a considerable minority of adolescents undergo psychosocial development along a route more characteristic of the other sex. Such variation confers a greater flexibility to both the individual and the community, reducing the common gender barrier of misunderstanding. This finding is crucial in responding to the criticism that boys and girls are naturally different and any attempt to soften these differences will lead to psychological disturbance and uncertain sexuality. Many schools include within their Personal and Social Education programmes some all-girls sessions in order to enhance confidence and assertiveness among girls, not least in dealing with the demands of boys. More rarely, but increasingly, all-boys sessions are being devoted to enhancing social sensitivity and providing a forum for boys to voice personal anxieties. Such work does not meet universal approval from parents who express concern that the children are undergoing a form of social engineering which will confuse them. The evidence relating to psychological androgyny allows one to deny that these activities are likely to be damaging the young.

Gender Differences in Identity

Is the concept of identity equally applicable to males and females? In broad terms we have seen that identity encompasses three key components, a description of self, a programme for one's future, and a sense of personal worthwhileness. Clearly the content of any of these components may vary. In many cultures the programme for the future, to take one example, will differ with gender, as career opportunities and social expectations vary. Nevertheless, it is difficult to conceive of a situation in which these three components are not central to adult functioning, regardless of gender, and to that extent the concept of identity is applicable to all.

More detailed examination of these three components may reveal gender differences. For example, it is not clear whether the three are given equal weighting by men and women, and whether they develop in the same sequence in adolescence. This territory has not been extensively researched. One exception is Kamptner (1988) who reports a psychometric study of approximately 400 students which revealed that for both males and females the descriptive and existential elements of identity linked with several family and social variables. There was, however, a marked gender difference relating to the programmatic element, despite the fact that the mean scores for this item were much the same. With males this element was also correlated with these variables, but with females the programmatic element seemed to be a free-standing, independent personality characteristic, a finding suggesting some different psychological processes are operating.

One area which has been studied more extensively is that of self-image, the descriptive component of identity. Although men and women have an equal overall sense of self-esteem, adolescent girls and adult women tend to be less confident than their male counterparts. There are also gender differences in what are seen to be the positive elements about the self. Females tend to mention their social qualities, such as their display of sympathy and willingness to work in cooperation, while males mention competitive qualities, their ambition, drive and practicality. These findings demonstrate the importance of socialization into gender roles. Women will mention their social skills as a positive feature but there is no evidence that as adolescents or adults females are more sociable than males. What is true is that females operate in social environments in which these social qualities are valued, and in turn the individual values them in herself.

It is difficult to better the words of Douvan and Adelson (1966) who made a study of 3000 American adolescents and concluded:

> The key terms for the adolescent development for a boy in our culture are the erotic, autonomy (assertiveness, independence, achievement) and identity. For the girls, the comparable terms are the erotic, the interpersonal and identity. Differences between the two sets of problems are larger and more complex than the single discrepancy implies; for this discrepancy is so central that it reverberates through the entire complex. (pp. 347–48)

If we look at Erikson's (1968) initial writing about gender and identity we find that he showed considerable ambiguity with respect to female development. He started his famous, and controversial essay on *Womanhood and the Inner Space* by stating his belief that modern society may benefit from assuming some more feminine qualities. He suggested that in an age of nuclear weapons male aggression needed some moderating influence and, with great sensitivity and prescience, argued that the equal opportunities movement should not lead to women attempting to compete with men by masculine criteria, but offer a valid feminine alternative. When, however, he moved on to describe the origins of masculine and feminine qualities the doubts arise.

In observing 300 children, aged ten to twelve years, playing with toys, Erikson noted consistent gender differences. Boys tended to build tall structures and most of the people and animals were placed outside the structure. Dynamic qualities were introduced into the play with cars moving around and being involved in collisions. In fact, much of the play involved risk-taking, with many of the tall structures collapsing in ruins. Girls tended to build structures which encompassed space, such as a room, and people and animals were placed inside this space. They were passive and there was little movement involved in the play. Although these beings were protected by being within the structure, the protective wall was not a very effective barrier and the possibility of intruders was considered, without much alarm.

These differences were attributed by Erikson to different body-images and developing sense of sex-roles, with the girls being aware of the importance of their body interior to reproduction, which in turn governed their identity. Whereas boys had to go out into the world and to gain their sense of identity through that experience, girls had to wait passively for a male to relate to them.

The first line of criticism relates to Erikson's initial observations. He built his description of gender differences around one strand of evidence, that of children's play, and some replication studies, for example by Caplan (1979), failed to detect the differences which he described. Nevertheless, we often can observe some gender differences in play, albeit not exactly those described by Erikson, but these differences may well arise from children being given different toys. Girls will be encouraged to play with dolls' houses while boys will be given model cars. Boys will be allowed to be more robust in their play. Boys and girls are thus socialized into different play behaviour.

We might also agree with Erikson that adolescents have a keen awareness of their developing bodies and sexuality. Boys and girls develop a different sense of body image, with the males having a sharper sense of a body-boundary, that which separates self from the outside world. To this extent we can go along with Erikson's description, it is in the interpretation of such findings that Erikson proved controversial.

He seems not to have emancipated himself from Freud's belief that 'biology is destiny', for he started his analysis of the children's play with a question:

> But how does the identity formation of women differ by dint of the fact that their somatic design harbors an 'inner space' destined to bear the offspring of chosen men and, with it, a biological, psychological and ethical commitment to take care of human infancy? (Erikson, 1968, p. 266)

The very form of the question assumes that this quality of the female body determines identity. Erikson saw his model being more positive to women than that of Freud, as unlike the latter he did not focus on a negative quality, the absence of a penis, but a positive quality, the possession of a 'vital inner potential'. Nevertheless, the model is still that of biological determinism. Furthermore, his interpretation lends itself to the criticism, often made of Freudians, that if you seek sexual symbolism then you are almost certain to find it, as almost any play or arrangement of toys can be described in terms of male genitalia, or female genitalia, or sexual intercourse.

The second concern with Erikson's model, and here the link with Freud is clearly apparent, is that it seems to perpetuate the view that males can exercise choice while females can only be passive and hope to be chosen. If the development of a personal identity involves making crucial choices, and it is difficult to envisage it being otherwise, then one can infer from the model that female identity is less developed. The possibility of a female developmental route as a valid alternative to that of the male is not considered.

A counter argument is that the biological ability of women to have children does not narrow the range of choices in life, as Erikson suggested, but opens up a wider range than that available to males. In other words, the biological restriction is placed on males: because they cannot bear children they usually are denied the option of assuming the prime responsibility for the home and child-care and can only act as a wage earner. This reversed argument is probably nearer the truth in so far that it hints at the conflict widely experienced by women in wishing both to have a family and pursue a career. Certainly, any account of female development has to acknowledge the existence of possible conflict between these two sets of aims.

A further ambiguity in Erikson's model relates to possible gender differences in life span psychosocial development. His original description, based on the study of males, suggested that an individual needed a firm sense of personal identity before being able to enter a psychologically intimate relationship with another. Thus Erikson (1964) wrote,

> . . . identity proves itself strongest where it can take chances with itself. For this reason, love in its truest sense presupposes both identity and fidelity. . . . it is important to realize that only graduation from adolescence permits the development of that intimacy, the selflessness of joined devotion, which anchors love in mutual commitment. (p. 128)

The person without a secure sense of identity, Erikson argued, would feel threatened by a really close relationship, they would fear losing their tenuous hold on their own individuality. There is a contradiction in his description of female development, as he argues that identity is the precursor of intimacy, but that a female gains her identity through relating to a male, so presumably for her the capacity for intimacy must precede the acquisition of identity.

This confusion about possible gender differences in psychosocial development has been extensively discussed and researched with the accumulation of evidence challenging Erikson's views on female development. Even older studies on all-male populations produced ambiguous results. For example, Orlofsky, Marcia and Lesser (1973) report a study of fifty-three college students which suggested that those who have achieved an identity may also maintain an intimate relationship, and identity diffusion subjects will not enjoy such a relationship, but the pattern was not simple as moratorium subjects were capable of psychological intimacy.

Hodgson and Fischer (1979) found a more complex pattern in their study of fifty male and fifty female college students. A greater proportion of females had reached intimacy, and for them the relationship with identity status was not clear cut. The following extracts from their·discussion section conveys their conclusions:

> Although the findings in this study tend to support Erikson's outline for male adolescent and young adult development, some evidence seems to criticize his version of female development. . . . men tend to resolve certain part conflicts earlier (i.e. occupational and political/religious ideology), but do not resolve the sexual ideology part conflict sooner than women . . . female identity development . . . follows different pathways . . . issues of intimacy are intertwined in female identity development in ways not adequately recognized by Erikson. (pp. 48–9)

Further complexities were suggested by Craig-Bray, Adams and Dobson (1988) in a study of forty-eight college students. They drew attention to the importance of same-sex intimate friends in supplying a confidant and a source of support. They suggested that same-sex and other-sex intimate friendships needed to be considered in building a picture of social development. Finally, they conclude: 'notions of identity and intimacy formation may be more psychologically integrated constructs for women than for men' (p. 186).

Research data can be interpreted in different ways, as illustrated by a study I carried with over 500 seventeen-year-old school students. The publication of a questionnaire by Rosenthal, Gurney and Moore (1981) made it possible to work with such a large number of subjects. The population was drawn from schools, rather than from colleges like most other studies, in an attempt to gain access to a wider ability range, even though this group was still skewed in favour of the academic achievers. The questionnaire contained twelve items relating to each construct, that of identity and that of intimacy. Using a score of nine, out of twelve, to provide the cut-of point, the population can be divided into those who have and those who have not achieved on each scale, as shown in *Table 2.*

Table 2:   Identity and intimacy achievement

	%
Males (274 subjects)	
Achieved neither	19
Achieved identity, but not intimacy	30
Achieved intimacy, but not identity	12
Achieved both	38
Females (282 subjects)	
Achieved neither	20
Achieved identity, but not intimacy	24
Achieved intimacy, but not identity	25
Achieved both	31

(As measured by Rosenthal, Gurney and Moore (1981) questionnaire among 17-year-old British youth.)

If we just look at the figures relating to males it seems at first sight that Erikson's model is vindicated. One sub-group, composed of those who have achieved intimacy but not identity, is incompatible with this model, but only 12 per cent of the population lie in this group, and such a small proportion can be attributed to a mix of text error and deviancy. Erikson's description, it can be argued, holds good for nearly 90 per cent of the population, and surely that is an acceptable fit for a psychological model. When we move on to look at the data for females some doubts must arise, for here the discrepant population accounts for 25 per cent of the total, too large a proportion to be dismissed so lightly.

We might look at the data in a different way. Hitherto, we have implicitly accepted Erikson's model, by assuming all those who have achieved neither quality, and all those who have achieved both, are compatible with his model. In fact, we have no way of knowing how those who have not achieved either identity or intimacy will develop. Likewise, we have no evidence about the developmental route which had been pursued by those who have achieved both identity and intimacy. We should disregard both these populations in this exercise. In this event, if we look at the female data, we see that slightly more than half of the population, 25 per cent compared to 24 per cent, were not developing along the lines postulated by Erikson. Unless we are going to adopt some extraordinary posture of suggesting that more than half the female population are deviant, we must concede that there exists a viable developmental route in which intimacy precedes identity. Furthermore, the data relating to males indicates that a considerable minority, 12 per cent compared to 30 per cent, follow the same route. To sum up, a careful examination of such data reveals that about 70 per cent of the males and just under 50 per cent of the females achieve identity prior to intimacy and the rest follow the alternative sequence.

Before we rely too much on one strand of evidence we need to scrutinize it for possible error. One problem is that we are imposing a scoring rule with a sharp cut-off on what is essentially continuous data. What will happen if achievement is attributed to a score of eight or ten, rather than nine? These possibilities have been checked. Obviously, the actual figures change, but the overall pattern is much the same, confirming the robustness of the evidence. Another concern is that a questionnaire may fail to separate foreclosure responses from those of achievement. Checks on the overall distribution of scores and on items which we might anticipate receiving a foreclosed response do not suggest that foreclosed subjects have been placed in the achievement category. In setting up the initial questionnaire the authors validated it against clinical categorization. Overall, it is reasonable to assume that the findings are valid.

In this event, we need to recognize the existence of a viable alternative developmental route to that postulated by Erikson, an alternative commoner among females, but existing with a minority of males. A question which we cannot answer with confidence is why there should be a lack of symmetry between the sexes. Surely, it might be argued, the minority of each sex, who follow the path characteristic of the other sex, should be of the same magnitude. The only answer I can offer is that the social pressure on males to conform to their stereotypical gender roles is greater than that on females, and such pressures could account for the empirical evidence of males forming a more homogeneous group. We might ask about the minorities. Are those who show some characteristics of the other sex disadvantaged? I interviewed a small number of teenagers who, on the basis of their test scores, fell into these minorities and did nor detect any problems. On the contrary, they seemed to be a mature and confident group, a finding which tends to confirm the claims made for psychological androgyny.

Gender Differences in Adolescence

After an extended consideration in this chapter of theoretical models of how gender differences develop and how they influence identity development we can return to the central issue of heterogeneity among adolescents.

In many respects the two sexes are more apart in early adolescence than at any other time in life. In addition to the life long factors of living in a gendered society and in having different experiences in being mothered, other issues contribute to the separation. As will be discussed in the next chapter, the experience of puberty is different in several respects for boys and girls. Girls mature much earlier, so there is a time in a class of twelve to thirteen-year-old pupils when girls are the physically dominating group. Alongside this physical change goes mental maturation, so girls begin to complain about the relative immaturity of the boys and prefer to keep company with other girls.

The experience of puberty is different in the sense that for boys it is in itself usually non-problematic (Gaddis and Brooks-Gunn, 1985), but for girls menstruation is a major cause of distress. Again, this point will be amplified in the next chapter. The important distinction is for boys, the experience of puberty is seen to add to the pleasures of life and they seek sexual activities to enhance this pleasure. For girls the experience of menstruation, and the fear of unwanted pregnancy, makes them more thoughtful and ambivalent about their sexual development, and they see the boys as being immature and exploitive in seeking sex.

After puberty boys and girls are treated differently by adults. Boys are allowed to spend much of their leisure time outside the home in the belief that they are now able to look after themselves. Girls are seen to be more at risk, now that they are sexually mature, and tend to be restricted in their leisure pursuits. For girls what develops is the 'culture of the bedroom', a phrase which is not meant to have a sexual connotation, but describes the situation in which girls spend time together in each other's bedrooms talking and listening to music. Once this physical separation occurs each group develops its own norms of behaviour, making the experience of adolescence even more strongly gendered.

In addition, as we have already noted, early adolescence is marked by commitment to the same-sex peer group. Particularly within the boys group conformity is enforced and it is essential to project a macho image and scorn that which is feminine, and this social pressure inhibits the making of friendships with girls. The argument derived from identity theory, that many boys find it difficult to enter psychologically intimate relationships before they have achieved a reasonable sense of their own identity, suggests that they will tend to delay the making of such relationships. Certainly, the evidence is that adolescent girls often prefer the company of older males, while the boys are still hesitant whether their prime loyalties are to their male mates or not.

The combination of these various effects is so powerful that most accounts of adolescence treat males and females as two distinct populations, and this distinction is maintained in reporting research evidence. Are other social variables, such as race and class, so powerful? Obviously, the question of salience, which in turn is dependent on context, arises. However, observation of friendship patterns among adolescents reveals that gender seems to be the dominant point of distinction. For example, boys of different ethnic origins will

> **Activity**
> Direct enquiries about their social life may seem intrusive but if you work with adolescents you can enquire how they spend their leisure time, who they are with and what they do. From the replies you can estimate the salience of such variables as race, class and gender, and also note the gender differences. How do these accounts compare with your memories of your own adolescence?

be playing football together in one area of the playground while an equally mixed group of girls will be clustered elsewhere. In some sections of this book, for example relating to employment, the class and ethnicity aspects are sufficiently important to demand specific attention. In other respects, such as sexuality, the interaction of gender with ethnicity may be important, but ethnicity in itself is less of an issue.

Chapter Summary

- Gender has been selected as the focus for the chapter as being important in itself and in providing an audit of our thinking about adolescents, in recognizing heterogeneity;
- gender differences develop prior to adolescence, through the gendered nature of society and the different experiences boys and girls have of their primary caretaker;
- in adolescence the different rates of maturation, attitudes toward sexual activity, and treatment by adults makes gender differences more salient;

- sex, gender and sexuality need to be distinguished, and the encouragement of psychological androgyny relates only to gender, and does not affect sexuality;
- both Freud and Erikson accepted a degree of biological determinism which yielded an inadequate account of female identity development;
- it seems commoner for males to need to develop a sense of personal identity before being able to enter a psychologically intimate relationship, but with females the capacity for such relationships tends to develop earlier.

Further Reading

ADAMS, G.R., GULLOTTA, T.P. and MONTEMAYOR, R. (Eds) (1992) *Adolescent Identity Formation*, Newbury Park, CA: Sage. Some chapters in this book address gender differences.

ASKEW, S. and ROSS, C. (1988) *Boys Don't Cry: Boys and Sexism in Education*, Milton Keynes: Open University Press. Still one of the best books on this topic.

CHODOROW, N. (1978) *The Reproduction of Mothering*, Berkeley: University of California Press. The prime authority arguing for the social reproduction of gender roles.

EOC/OFSTED (1996) *The Gender Divide: Performance Differences Between Boys and Girls at School*, London: HMSO. Essentially a government consultation paper inviting responses.

MURPHY, P. and GIPPS, C. (Eds) (1996) *Equity in the Classroom*, London: Falmer Press. Based on a UNESCO symposium and contains a wide ranging collection of papers on gender issues.

SALISBURY, J. and JACKSON, D. (1996) *Challenging Macho Values: Practical Ways of Working with Adolescent Boys*, London: Falmer Press. One of the few texts which contains practical suggestions for work with adolescents.

WEINER, G. and ARNOT, M. (Eds) (1987) *Gender Under Scrutiny: New Inquiries in Education*, London: Unwin Hyman. An interesting collection.

Chapter 5

Sexual Behaviour and Relationships

Any account of adolescence has to recognize the centrality of the physical changes associated with puberty and the growing importance of sexuality to the individual. Additionally, there have been dramatic changes in public attitudes and values in the last few decades, so that the task for the young person of adjusting to the prevailing norms and establishing an adult status has, in turn, altered equally dramatically. Failure to recognize the extent and pace of the social change can inhibit adult understanding of contemporary youth.

Changing Attitudes and Behaviour

The process of social change commenced at the beginning of the 1960s, with the famous court case in which D.H. Lawrence's novel *Lady Chatterley's Lover* was judged not to be obscene and could be legally sold in this country. Prior to this case Britain had maintained particularly strict censorship with respect to alleged pornography but the new legal precedent brought Britain in line with most other European countries. In the middle of the decade, the post of Lord Chamberlain, who censored the theatre, was abolished. The regime had been so severe that a modern classic such as Arthur Miller's *A View from the Bridge* was banned because one man kissed another in one scene. Such behaviour was judged likely to incite homosexual passions at a time when all male homosexual contact was illegal. The irony was that in the play the kiss was not motivated by erotic interest but by a wish of one man to humiliate the other.

In 1967 parliamentary changes to the law legalized abortion and male homosexual acts, although in the case of the latter there remained various restrictions, notably the high age of consent of twenty-one. At the same time the availability of the birth control pill transformed the sexual behaviour of young people. The greater freedom in respect to sexual behaviour was paralleled by greater openness in the press and on television in their coverage of these issues.

Although uneven, this move towards a more permissive society has continued. A more recent example is that prior to the advent of HIV/AIDS schools often offered little advice about birth control techniques, mainly for fear of offending certain religious groups. With the current emphasis on safe sex practices specific information has to be given and detailed advice about the use of condoms is provided. Contrast the current situation, with condoms openly on sale in every supermarket and high street chemist, with that of Cambridge in the 1950s as described by Tom Sharpe in his novel *Porterhouse Blue*. At that time, condoms were only available from under the counter in rather louche chemists and hairdressers and Sharpe tells of the efforts of a shy undergraduate to purchase some. All his efforts were thwarted by some circumstance, such as someone from his own College being in the same shop. Contemporary youth miss the humour in this book as they find this story totally bewildering.

One final example is that currently attention has been given to the case of a magazine aimed for teenage girls which gave detailed and precise advice on how to carry out fellatio. Various voices have questioned whether this material is suitable for such a magazine, but even ten years ago nothing similar would have been published.

What has happened has been a total change in the public discourse and behaviour. On balance most of us will probably welcome the change in the former. There are many accounts of ignorance causing unnecessary distress to youth in the past, for example with a girls thinking that menstruation signalled some severe illness and boys believing that masturbation led to insanity. In the words of George Steiner: 'To grow up after Freud is to be liberated from a whole spectre host of unnecessary terrors, hypocrisies and idolatries'.

However, Foucault (1979), in his history of sexuality, reminds us that talk can constrain people as well as free them. An obvious example is that in the past two people of the same sex living together might have been seen as not having a sexual relationship, even if in reality they were. Nowadays it would be believed that they were in such a relationship, even if that is not the case. We have become more aware, more knowing, and that can constrain.

The effects of this greater openness on young people are complicated. They are better informed but, at the same time, they are more likely to have a sense of sexual norms to which they believe that they ought to adhere. A failure to have a sexual relationship, and to have sexual intercourse of a certain frequency and duration, may lead to social ridicule and personal distress. In counselling adolescents today one key point which has to be made is that, as in all aspects of living, there is a natural diversity in sexual interests and behaviour, and they should feel content in being themselves and not feel pressurized to conform to some, possibly mythical, norm. From my experience of counselling I am tempted to suggest that half of the male teenage population fear that they are over-sexed, being obsessive, while the other half fear that they might in some way be deficient or under-sexed.

The changes in behaviour can be more readily quantified. Schofield (1965) in a major study of the sexual behaviour of young people in Britain found that 11 per cent of the boys aged 15–17 had experience of sexual intercourse and for the corresponding girls it was 6 per cent. Among 17–19-year-olds the incidence was 30 per cent for males and 16 per cent for females.

Table 3: Percentage of women and men who had their first experience of sexual intercourse prior to the age of sixteen, shown by age at interview (the data was collected in 1990–91)

Age at interview	Women %	Men %
16–19	18.7	27.6
20–24	14.7	23.8
25–29	10.0	23.8
30–34	8.6	23.2
35–39	5.8	18.4
40–44	4.3	14.5
45–49	3.4	13.9
50–54	1.4	8.9
55–59	0.8	5.8

Source: WELLINGS, K., FIELD, J., JOHNSON, A.M. and WADSWORTH, J. (1994) *Sexual Behaviour in Britain*, London: Penguin.

A major, recent study of sexual behaviour in Britain reveals that the median age for young men and women, aged 16 to 19, to have had their first experience of intercourse is now seventeen, three or four years earlier than reported by people in their fifties (Wellings *et al.*, 1994).

One important aspect of the contemporary figures is that about one fifth of girls and over a quarter of the boys have their first sexual experience prior to the age of sixteen, the age of being deemed able to give consent. *Table 3*, based on Wellings *et al.* (1992, p. 42), shows how these figures contrast with those obtained from older people. This situation has raised both ethical and legal difficulties for those providing assistance with contraception to those under sixteen. Despite the widespread availability of birth control devices known pregnancy among girls aged under sixteen remains high, at about 7 300 in 1993 (Central Statistical Office, 1996). Of these, 3 500 proceeded to maternity and 3 800 had an abortion. The government's Health of the Nation Targets for the year 2000 aims to reduce pregnancy of girls under sixteen to 4 800.

Schofield (1965) found that 5 per cent of the males and 16 per cent of the females, aged 16 to 19, admitted that they had not enjoyed intercourse, and 12 per cent of the males and 29 per cent of the females reported that they never, or only rarely, had an orgasm under these circumstances. These findings caused him to comment:

> Adults who criticise teenage morality always seem to assume that sexual intercourse is irresistible unless some form of restraint is in the way. These figures show other factors may be at work. Group pressures or a desire to be thought experienced and worldly may persuade some teenagers to take part in sexual intercourse although they do not really enjoy it; there may be strong pressures upon a boy to prove his masculinity, and upon a girl from the fear that she may lose the boys if she does not agree to intercourse. (p. 91)

More recent evidence supports his hypotheses. Lees (1986) confirms the fact that tremendous pressure is put on adolescent girls by their male peers to agree to sexual intercourse. Studies of early male experience indicates that this pressure comes more from a wish to establish a high status with other males than in being emotionally involved with the partner. In fact, many boys report that while they are having sex they are thinking about their male friends, not in a homoerotic sense, but anticipating being able to tell their friends about that success, 'If only my friends could see me now' (Holland *et al.*, 1993, p. 19). For these boys sexual intercourse is a rite-of-passage, a hurdle on the road to adulthood which has to be conquered. Given that boys have this agenda we can see why the hope of girls that sex will strengthen the relationship will often be disappointed.

One young man commented: 'I think from a bloke's point of view they are not so bothered like who they lose their virginity to, or who they sleep with, and I think to a girl, or woman it means much more' (Holland *et al.*, 1993, p. 21).

The conclusion that we can reach is that although adolescents today are better informed and gain earlier experience than their predecessors, their sexual development remains subject to social pressures, contradictions and misunderstanding as ever.

> **Activity**
> Purchase copies of magazines aimed at teenage girls and analyse the ways issues of sexual behaviour are covered. Note the extent of coverage, the range of issues discussed, and what moral stance, if any, which comes through in the writing. (There are no comparable magazines for boys, they tend to read either emotionally neutral material, on football, cars or fishing, or purchase soft adult pornography).

Gender Differences in Approach to Sexuality

A combination of the social and the biological act to make gender differences so significant so that more than in any other aspect of adolescent development the response to the developing sexuality differs with gender. This distinction reflects the old dual morality, in which males were seen to be, and encouraged to be, sexually active, while females of the same age were not. This traditional belief failed to recognize that women might welcome sexual activity, so although men could claim 'conjugal rights', there was no equivalent concept applying to women. The fact that female homosexuality has never been specifically a subject of legal constraint, in contrast to the situation with males, reflects the belief that women will not take a sexual initiative and their only role is to respond to a man. Although social attitudes to females' sexuality have changed immensely in recent years, women are still likely to be stigmatized for being sexually active and often have to cope with a consequent pregnancy on their own.

Alongside these differing social expectations there are the biological factors. The most extensive study of physical development in children and adolescents was undertaken by Tanner and his associates, and although the

Figure 5:   Gender Differences in the Timing of Puberty, shown by Growth Spurt

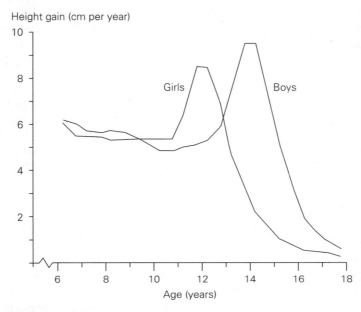

Source: TANNER, J.M. (1962) *Growth at Adolescence,* Oxford: Blackwell.

data is no longer new and puberty is ever occurring at an earlier age, the over-all developmental patterns are likely to be similar. *Figure 5* shows the effect of puberty on the growth spurt in height. In the first year of life the infant grows by about twenty-two cm. The rate then decreases to about five to six cm per annum until the onset of puberty. As the diagram shows, girls develop about two years earlier than the boys, but for the latter the growth spurt is more pronounced and extended, so eventually the boys will tend to overtake the girls. These measures of height are indicative of a whole host of bodily changes, both external in appearance, and internal in the hormonal environment. The two-year lead by girls is reflected in the marked difference in maturity, both physical and mental.

A further difference is in the experience of puberty. Prendergast (1992) reports a study of over 500 girls with over 80 per cent reporting feeling pain, fatigue, heavy bleeding and irritability with menstruation, and between 49 per cent and 65 per cent said each of these symptoms occurred almost always. Given the extent of these unpleasant experiences it can be appreciated why female adolescents feel ambiguous about their physical development, to the extent that some slip into anorexia in an attempt to alleviate the effects. There is no corresponding problem for boys and most report the first experience of ejaculation to be pleasurable and welcome in confirming their maturation (e.g. Gaddis and Brooks-Gunn, 1985).

The problems for boys arise less from puberty itself, but more from its delay. The late developing boy is physically weaker than his peers and cannot compete effectively at sports or in a fight. The only possible weapon within the competitive peer group is that of verbal wit, often small boys employ that tool, but it can alienate others and increase his isolation. What starts as differences in physiological development extends into the psychological. Josselson, Greenberger and McConochie (1977) reported:

> Whereas the high-maturity boys derive self-esteem from what they do and from internalized objects, the low-maturity boys rely on the approval of their friends to gain a sense of self-worth. Similarly, the high-maturity boys demonstrate a struggle for self-definition and self-knowledge in focusing on what they are to become while the low-maturity boys remain present-orientated and express themselves primarily in action which serves immediate needs. (p. 45)

The gender differences in response to puberty, with boys tending to see sexual activity solely as a source of pleasure while girls are more aware of the matrix of issues involved, affects behaviours. The simplistic approach of many boys causes them to ignore the possible consequences of sexual activity, for example by refusing to use a condom to prevent conception on the grounds 'that is not my problem — it is hers'. With the advent of HIV/AIDS we might expect a more sensible response, but Hill (1995) reports that even young men aged 16 to 18 in further education showed a cavalier attitude. One youth said 'Never had sex with a condom; never wore one. . . . what do you need condoms for if you can pull out in time . . . ?' (p. 237). It is sad that such ignorance was commonly accompanied by an arrogance which made the men among this student group resist education about AIDS on the basis they knew all about it already. Given these attitudes, it is not surprising that many adolescent girls prefer to go out with older men, finding the immaturity of their male contemporaries irritating. Eventually, young men do mature and relationships between contemporaries improves.

Homosexuality: Identity, Behaviour and Attitudes

In a recent British survey, Wellings *et al.* (1993) reveal that only 5.2 per cent of the men and 2.7 per cent of the women interviewed admitted to having had any homosexual experience. Given that we are only dealing with a small minority it may seem odd to devote a whole sub-section of this book to the topic. There are two reasons for this decision: there is ample evidence that the issue of homosexuality is of concern to many adolescents, and the topic strikingly illuminates many of the factors which impinge on our response to sexuality.

Nowhere else has the change in public discourse been so apparent. From what was called 'the love that dares not speak its name', we have a culture in which it seems as if every play or novel has a gay character in it. Yet, despite this heightened awareness, prejudice remains strong, expressed by failing to recognize female homosexuality and hostility to it among males.

Prejudice against homosexual behaviour is deep rooted in Jewish and Christian cultures, drawing support from both Testaments of the Bible. In the Middle Ages sodomy was seen by the Church to be an act of Devil worship alongside the celebration of the Black Mass. But despite such beliefs there was in practice little attempt to suppress homosexual behaviour until the late nineteenth century. In Britain the Labouchere Amendment of 1886, making all sexual contacts between males illegal, represented the formal expression of this attitude change. Within society there were major changes in perception. When the word *homosexual* was first coined in the middle of that century it was used as an adjective to describe an act or a behaviour, but by the end of the century it was also used as a noun, to describe a person. This point may seem pedantic but its significance might be illustrated by analogy. If any one of us is described as having acted in a mean way on a particular occasion then, although we may not like the comment, we can live with it. Most people would admit to lacking generosity in some situation. If, however, we are described as being a miser then I suspect most people would find the term insulting and threatening. We are now labelled as having some consistent characteristic which is undesirable. The existence of such a persistent trait suggests there may be some innate character defect. We are no longer talking of a behaviour which is within the compass of all of us, but of a person who is pathological. Likewise when the word homosexual was being used as an adjective it described a particular act or event, which was in the potential repertoire of everyone. When used as noun the word carries the connotation of a pathology, a syndrome, which immediately suggested a clinical condition requiring some form of treatment or cure. This change of attitude in the nineteenth century has been attributed in Foucault's (1979) thesis to an exercise in social control.

Over the next fifty years the law was enforced with intermittent stringency, but in the early 1950s there was a further period of increased constraint. One disturbing feature at that time was what courts would accept as decisive evidence, as shown in an infamous case involving the trial in 1954 of three men, including a well-known peer (Wildeblood, 1955). These men were convicted and sent to prison solely on the basis of evidence provided by their partners, who were adult and had freely consented to the activities. These informants were not themselves charged for their admitted sexual behaviour. The fact that courts would accept uncorroborated evidence from an accomplice in this fashion set homosexual behaviour apart from other criminal offences, where more substantial evidence would be required for conviction, and opened up endless opportunities for blackmail. In the event, public reaction to such cases led to the reform in the Sexual Offences Act of 1967.

Harassment has continued. For example the seizure in the 1980s from an openly gay, but totally respectable, bookshop in London of books by writers such as Andre Gide, Kate Millet and Tennessee Williams which were readily available in bookshops all over London. Despite Home Office attempts to stop the practice, plain clothes police have acted as *agents provocateurs*, engaging in conversation which may lead to an arrest for importuning. The status of homosexuality remains ambiguous, as shown by this comment by Mrs Thatcher as Prime Minister to the 1987 Conservative Party Conference, that people did not have an 'inalienable right' to be homosexual. It might be argued that people have precisely that right, to develop and live out their identity, except where it leads specifically to illegal behaviour.

This extensive prejudice impinges on adolescents in several ways. It condones homophobia within their own circles and makes it incredibly difficult for the young person who is uncertain about their sexuality to discuss their feelings. One problem is the lack of a role model. Many groups of people are oppressed, often by virtue of qualities such as race, but they possess the reassurance that they are not alone. The problems are shared with the family and friends. The teenager can find adults within the same class or race who can be respected, who, by their example, demonstrate that it is possible to lead a satisfactory life despite the social pressures. Adolescents who think that they may be homosexual often believe themselves to be unique. They are not aware of being acquainted with anyone who shares their concern. The only persons they recognize as being homosexual is someone displaying the extreme stage stereotype, the highly masculine woman or highly effeminate man. They cannot identify with this person and consequently do not see how they fit into society.

There are particular difficulties in counselling young people about their sexuality. With males aged less than eighteen there is the problem that homosexual activity is illegal for them, and counselling agencies are reluctant to suggest anything which might be construed as a recommendation to break the law. Furthermore, Clause 28 of the Local Government Act 1988 specifically forbids the 'promotion' of homosexuality. No one is clear what constitutes 'promotion' in this context, but many bodies, including the educational services, may prefer to ignore situations involving homosexuality in order to avoid any charge of contravening this Act. Consequently, the adolescent is isolated from the family and friends and feels very vulnerable. Trenchard and Warren (1984) point out that about a fifth of the gay adolescents in their sample had seriously considered suicide.

Why is this prejudice against homosexuality so strong? There are two possible causal factors. Identity theory reveals that it is the foreclosed person who is most intolerant, and in a sense prejudice breeds prejudice, as an adult who foreclosed on his or her sexuality will create an emotional climate in which youngsters are likely to follow the same route. Secondly, no one can prove what their sexual orientation might be. An accusation cannot be readily refuted, so many feel vulnerable. This situation among adolescents is vividly described by Nayak and Kehily (1996). One boy in school said that he had seen a film about AIDS which contained a gay character. Another boy then said: 'And you sat and watched it?' which led to a revealing response: 'We had to! We had to sit and watch it, we had no choice, we had to stay there and watch it' (p. 222). Note that the comment about sitting and watching the film amounted to an accusation, of either of being a wimp in submitting to such an indignity or being covertly interested in the topic. The strength of the denial by the other boys testifies to the impact this accusation had on him. The same authors noted that teenage boys were obviously inspired by horror films in reacting to suspected homosexuality among their peers by making the sign of a crucifix with their fingers, as if to exorcise evil spirits.

A further complicating factor is that there is not always congruence between sexual identity and behaviour. In some cultures it is not uncommon for young unmarried men to participate in homosexual activity if they have no access to women. It has been a problem with AIDS education in this context as the men do not identify themselves as being gay, and do not recognize the applicability of advice about AIDS to them.

The relationship between having a sense of a homosexual identity and actual physical experience has been extensively researched, for example, by Coyle (1988). The situation is complicated, some men and women report recognizing that they knew themselves to be 'different' long before puberty, while others only gained realization well into adulthood. Possibly, if both the sense of gender and sexuality are atypical then the young person recognizes the situation, but when someone is totally at ease with their gender roles then their unusual sexual orientation may be less easily recognized. People in the latter category may start by living as a heterosexual but then find, against their will, other interests developing. One thing is clear, there is no support for the seduction theory, that homosexual experience will turn everyone into being orientated that way. Consensual sexual experiences tend to confirm the underlying psychology, some will find an experience unrewarding, for others it can be a revelation. There is however, evidence that both boys and girls who have been abused and experienced rape are likely to suffer subsequently from a range of stress symptoms (Finkelhor, 1990).

The complexity of the situation is revealed by Kitzinger (1987) who in a study of lesbian women identifies five sub-groups:

1   Those who reported a sense of personal fulfilment, feeling free and comfortable with their sexuality.
2   Others argued that the crucial variable was the quality of the person one loved, rather than their biological sex. In other words, these women did not see themselves as being lesbian, but being within a lesbian relationship at this moment in their life. Many in this group saw themselves as being bisexual.
3   Women in this group outwardly conformed with the predominately heterosexual norms of society and kept their lesbianism secret.
4   Women in this group felt that their sexuality had politicized them so they were now active in a wider range of feminist initiatives.
5   Some women had a rather negative self-image and saw themselves suffering because of their sexual orientation.

What can we do to help adolescents who are concerned about their sexual orientation? We should bear three points in mind. They may already have encountered considerable hostility and misunderstanding, and approach us in a state of despair and depression. We should not say anything to enhance such negative feelings. Second, although their homosexual interests may prove transitory, dismissing them as 'just a passing phase' may seem to the teenager that you are not taking them seriously. Third, if they tell us that they are already in a relationship then the same questions one asks about a heterosexual relationship apply, e.g. looking for evidence either of care and affection, or of coercion and exploitation. In any event, these young people should be treated with sensitivity, as the process of 'coming out', that is admitting to one's sexuality, is difficult enough without us compounding their anxieties in any way.

The Social Self and Sexual Self

One common error in thinking about adolescent sexual development is that attention is focused too much on physical activity and not enough on emotional needs. People seek a close relationship not only for physical satisfaction but for the emotional support some psychological intimacy can provide. Erikson defined the main psychosocial task of young adults as being able to enter a psychologically intimate relationship, one in which defences are lowered and emotional honesty is possible. We have seen that his sequential model, with identity achievement being a necessary prerequisite for such an intimate relationship, does not hold up for everyone, particularly females. It seems as if the search for identity and an intimate relationship commonly overlap in adolescence and early adulthood.

Unfortunately, just as young people are finding it easier to gain physical experience than in the past they are finding much less certainty and security associated with close relationships. In 1993, the marriage rate in Britain was 5.9 per thousand of the population while the corresponding divorce rate was 3.1. Remembering that about one third of all marriages are remarriages then the divorce rate was uncomfortably close to the rate of first marriages. Twenty two per cent of all families were headed by a single parent, compared with 8 per cent in 1971. Where, as is usual, the mother has custody of the children, then by two years after the divorce 40 per cent of the fathers have lost all contact with their children. A further social change is that commonly young people live together prior to marriage so the age at the time of the first marriage has risen to twenty-six for females and to twenty-eight for males. One final statistic, 32 per cent of all live births in 1994 were outside marriage, compared to 5 per cent in 1962.

What the figures, all gained from the Central Statistical Office (1996), show is that contemporary teenagers are growing up in a different social milieu from their predecessors. Many will have been brought up by a single parent. Under these conditions they may have suffered from immediate disadvantage, notably financial. It is difficult for a single parent to maintain a home, give adequate time to the children and earn a good salary, often one element has to be sacrificed. The children also suffer from a longer term disadvantage, as it is from living close to adults who are enjoying a close relationship that the young are most likely to learn how to enter such a relationship themselves. Chodorow argued that it is from the girl's experience of being mothered that she learns to become a mother, and we might extend this notion of social reproduction to cover the whole spectrum of family relationships. A personal sense of identity partly comes from comparing oneself with others, and the adolescent needs access to a range of other people to make such comparisons. In extreme cases the adolescent may have such a jaundiced view of family life that he or she will make no effort to develop long term relationships.

The area of debate can be widened further by recognizing that humans have a variety of social needs, and a sexual partner is only part of that matrix. We have in varying degrees the need to give and receive love, to act as mentors and as followers, to relate intellectually, socially and emotionally with others. One example of this social requirement comes from a recent study of stress among students studying to become school teachers (Head, Hill and Maguire, 1996). One of the groups expressing the highest stress was composed of males who were not involved in a close relationship. Presumably those within a relationship talk through their concerns with their partner and this process of articulating and sharing anxieties helped in their resolution. Unattached females seemed to network more effectively than the males so they could talk about emotionally explicit matters with their friends. Within male friendships much emotional expression is taboo.

Achieving an identity is not just concerned with sexuality but with our complete social self. We need to develop a self-image, and a life-programme, which accounts for the range of social relationships. The question of who erotically attracts us is part of a wider question of how we relate to a variety of people. In this event, it is a wider social identity which is the key, albeit the issue of sexual response is embedded within that concept.

What emerges from this discussion is the need to contextualize the issues in two ways. The first, and this point has been discussed at length, is to locate sexuality within the wider needs of the social self. The second, is to integrate the identity of the social self with other aspects of living. Vocational choices, for example, have implications for life-style and social life. Some employment requires one to meet and socialize with many people, other employment may involve considerable solitude. The successful acquisition of an identity involves recognizing how one operates as a social being, and then finding a way of living which allows this social need to operate alongside the requirements of work. Some balance is required. Loneliness can be depressing, but equally a frenetic social life inhibits thought and the development of self-knowledge. Storr (1988) has suggested that within our culture we tend to emphasize the virtues of companionship to the detriment of the autonomy which can lead to our most creative work. Identity achievement involves integrating these diverse claims on the self. Such integration has not only to occur pragmatically, but also existentially, in that the individual needs to feel that it adds up to a worthwhile and meaningful programme, and embedded in this matrix is the important, but not totally discrete issue of sexuality.

Helping Adolescents

Sexuality is notoriously a difficult area for adults to work with adolescents. In reviewing the literature, Moore and Rosenthal (1993) point out:

> Research about sources of sex information for adolescents shows overwhelmingly that peers are a major influence in this area, with parents playing a minor role in the sex education of their children . . . While it is certainly important for the young person who is establishing values and rehearsing for adult sexuality to have the sympathetic ear and counsel of friends, the sex education provided from this resource is limited and often is not supplemented by other sources . . . a case of 'the blind leading the blind'. (p. 67)

There are several barriers between adults in general, and parents in particular, and adolescents in this context. Parents are associated with the super-ego, the internalized moral code developed from parental control and strictures, such that it is difficult to imagine adults being sympathetic or understanding about sex. Many adolescents report that they cannot envisage their parents engaging in intercourse, a finding which raises interesting questions about their own conception. These barriers cannot be quickly broken down but we can at least prepare ourselves for participating more fully in the education of our children and students.

Activity
List the range of topics which might at some stage come within a sex education programme, including issues of abortion, contraception, AIDS and homosexuality. What do you think is the appropriate age for young people to encounter these various notions? Would you provide the same education for boys as for girls? If possible, compare your ideas with others. How effective would you be, in terms of competence (knowing enough about each issue) and confidence (not being embarrassed)? Do you know where you, or the adolescent, could gain further help, e.g. from various agencies and telephone lines?

Chapter Summary

- One recent social change has been a greater openness about sex, but this widening discourse can constrain as well as empower;
- there has been a corresponding change in behaviour with young people gaining sexual experience at an earlier age;
- there are social pressures on both boys and girls to enter sexual relationships;
- high divorce rates and conception rates outside marriage testify to the increased instability in personal relationships;
- boys mature physically and mentally much more slowly than girls so there is mismatch in interests and expectations between the sexes in early adolescence;
- our response to homosexuality and bisexuality reveals many issues related to sexual development, e.g. the relationship between behaviour and identity, and the extent of social pressure young people face.

Further Reading

Foucault, M. (1979, 1990) *The History of Sexuality: Volume One (1979), Volume Three (1990)*, Harmondsworth: Penguin. The whole series of books are worth reading and have had an immense influence on contemporary thought.

Holland, J., Ramazanoglu, C. and Sharpe, S. (1993) *Wimp or Gladiator: Contradictions in Acquiring Masculine Sexuality*, London: Tufnell Press. A brief booklet, but contains revealing first-hand accounts.

Lees, S. (1986) *Losing Out: Sexuality and Adolescent Girls*, London: Hutchinson. A rich collection of accounts by the girls.

Moore, S. and Rosenthal, D. (1993) *Sexuality in Adolescence*, London: Routledge. A good survey, but more of the empirical evidence comes from Australia than Britain.

Trenchard, L. and Warren, H. (1984) *Something to Tell You*, London: Gay Teenager's Group. Contains a series of personal accounts of experiencing hostility and revealing the common fear of being thrown out of the family home.

Wellings, K., Field, J., Johnson, A.M. and Wadsworth J. (1994) *Sexual Behaviour in Britain: The National Survey of Attitudes and Lifestyles*, London: Penguin. More of a source book for information than providing a narrative, reporting a large-scale survey.

Chapter 6

Entering the World of Work

It has been a common criticism of Freud that, although he stated that happiness came from love and work, he did not spell out the function of work in this context. A parallel omission can be identified in much of contemporary psychology in which vocational guidance has developed as a discrete specialism without any regard for issues of identity development. Possibly the uncritical acceptance of two part-truths has encouraged this neglect.

The first belief is that career choice is made solely by regard to aptitudes. It can be argued that through schooling people come to identify their abilities and then, in the light of such recognition, the choices become obvious. Psychologists have made considerable effort to see whether measured aptitudes among students prove to be predictive of adult achievement. The results need careful interpretation. Certainly, it is true that for some specific careers the possession of intrinsic abilities is crucial. To become an opera singer an individual needs to be naturally endowed with a good voice combined with considerable musical and acting abilities, qualities which cannot be provided simply through good training. More generally, we find that most jobs demand some specific skills, so it is not true that everyone can do everything. Workers in vocational guidance have long recognized this instrumental need and have devised tests for abilities in fields such as mathematics, languages and visual design. There seems to exist a threshold and one cannot succeed without the minimum ability to pass that threshold, but many more people possess the necessary minimum ability than enter any particular form of employment. In that sense, the pool of potential talent is larger than the demand made on it, so although the lack of abilities can disqualify some people from succeeding in a particular career, the possession of the necessary abilities does not seem to be the sole determinant of career choice.

The other half-truth relates to the role of serendipity. Many adults will relate how some chance happening, or perhaps the example provided by a charismatic teacher, caused them to suddenly make a change in their career plans. A well recorded instance of such serendipity is reported in the case of W.H. Auden. At the age of fifteen he had been planning to enter some science-based career, perhaps as a mining engineer, until he had a chance conversation with a school contemporary, Robert Medley. Auden described the incident in these terms:

> One afternoon in March at half-past three
> When walking in a ploughed field with a friend;

Kicking a little stone, he turned to me
And said, 'Tell me do you write poetry?'
I never had, and said so, but I knew
That very moment what I wished to do.
(Reprinted from Mendeson, E. (Ed.) (1977) *The English Auden*, London,
Faber. Reprinted with permission) (Auden, 1936, p. 194)

Auden's account captures the surprise and suddenness of the decision, an event which could be set at a precise time and place. No one can doubt the significance of this moment to him.

The mistake is to assume that this chance conversation provided the cause for his decision, rather than it being a trigger for an underlying, but yet unrecognized, need. Suppose this conversation has never taken place. Would we then assume that Auden would never have become a poet? Suppose Medley had addressed the same question to half-a-dozen other boys in the school. Would we assume that all of them would have chosen to write poetry and have succeeded as well as Auden? All that a serendipitous event can do is to precipitate a decision which would probably have been made sooner or later in any event. Identity acquisition is too fundamental to be simply the product of chance.

The Importance of Career Choice

Erikson reinstated the importance of work, seeing success in this area, alongside the development of sexuality and an ideology, as part of the life task for the adolescent. In fact, he argued that the roots of vocational identity, to use his terminology, go back to the latency period, prior to adolescence. He wrote,

> . . . while all children need their hours and days of make-believe in games, they all, sooner or later, become dissatisfied and disgruntled without a sense of being able to make things and make them well and even perfectly, it is this that I have called the *sense of industry*. (Erikson, 1968, p. 123)

He develops this idea,

> Since industry involves doing things beside and with others, a first sense of the division of labor and of differential opportunity — that is, a sense of the *technological ethos* of a culture — develops at this time. Therefore, the configurations of culture and the manipulations basic to the *prevailing technology* must reach meaningfully into school life, supporting in every child a feeling of competence . . . (Erikson, 1968, p. 126)

These passages demonstrate how effective Erikson was in locating individual development within the cultural matrix.

He then suggested that in adolescence the issue of a vocational identity becomes crucial — 'In general it is the inability to settle on an occupational identity which most disturbs young people' (Erikson, 1968, p. 132). This latter claim needs some unpacking, not least because, as we must repeatedly remind ourselves, he was so male-centred in his analysis.

There can be no doubt that the achievement of an occupational identity is important at several levels. At a very pragmatic level employment provides the young person with some financial independence from the family, allowing greater freedom in the choice of how money should be spent.

Although gaining employment represents a step in achieving independence from the family it is a topic in which the adolescent will take note of advice from parents. At a time when relationships with parents can be strained, and when many adolescents will be most reluctant to discuss some issues of their personal development with the family, the search for a career provides an exception. In this context the parents are perceived to be a better guide than peers. The parents can exercise an influence in at least four ways. They can help develop interests and abilities by the choice of objects bought for the home, for example, books or a computer. They can, if able, provide direct coaching and skill training. They may act as role models and, finally, they can inhibit choice by rejecting some possibilities as being unsuitable for their child.

The perceptions of the adolescent held by others will change. The employed teenager has a higher social status among peers than those still at school, and the individual is credited with greater maturity. Employment also allows the adolescents to gain entry to the adult world and to be able to talk to adults on equal terms. The young person may only hold a very junior position in the place of work but, nevertheless, is part of the workforce, able to understand and discuss the concerns of the others, and thus enter into adult discourse. In this way, the adolescent has managed to pass from the awkward sense of being at 'the age between' (Miller, 1969) and enter into adulthood.

There are also gains in self-image and valuation. In part this concerns practical issues. The physical and emotional changes of adolescence can produce a feeling of a loss of control, and success in employment provides reassurance that one has a degree of competence. Knowing that one can cope with the demands of work aids the development of confidence which can help with the handling of other aspects of development. The combination of appropriate measures of competence and confidence make the young person an effective functioning being.

Alongside this pragmatic side goes the emerging existential need to do something worthwhile in life. Although many jobs only provide a limited innate sense of doing something worthwhile, at least the adolescent feels a start has been made, one is producing something or is providing a service, and is being paid to do so. Young people who chose careers for positive reasons, rather than just drifting into a job, probably do so for one of three reasons. Sometimes it was a very practical choice, made in the knowledge of personal strengths and weaknesses, in the light of the self-image. Others may be concerned with the potential benefits offered by a career, whether it will confer prestige and wealth. Clearly these adolescents are more influenced by the programmatic element. Finally, others will wish to be of service to the community, and will make a choice which allows the realization of such idealism. Clearly, these different purposes may suggest different career choices to the adolescent, who then has to decide on which factor is the more important, and act accordingly.

In terms of the overall psychological development vocational choice means that one of life's crucial choices has been made. If things work out satisfactorily it allows the adolescent the space and psychic energy to confront other aspects of the emerging identity. Usually the decision about a career is the first of the crucial life choices to be made. A child may not realize that issues of sexuality, particularly sexual orientation, can prove to be problematic, yet he or she will recognize that schooling only occurs for a finite time and then career choices have to be made. Consequently, adolescents have anticipated the need for making a choice in relation to work, and will have reached some conclusions, even though they may not yet see a practical solution. Often the role of the parent or the teacher is to help the adolescent bring coherence to their thoughts, so that the overall pattern can be seen, which in turn implies specific outcomes. Serendipity occurs because a chance event or comment may provide a sufficient catalyst for this mental reorganization.

Another feature of occupational choice is that it is public and must involve some degree of commitment. In other areas of identity development it is possible to remain at the diffusion stage for a long while and to conceal the situation from others, but when an adolescent enters employment the period of indecision and ambiguity is over, and a public statement is made to this effect. The decision may need to be explained and justified, and in so doing the young person is making one of their first statements about themselves as an autonomous adult being. There can be a considerable psychological investment in such a process. The contemporary uncertainty in the labour market has probably inhibited this effect so that the young can not invest so much of their sense of identity in gaining a permanent job.

We have seen that in making occupational choice the adolescent needs to take note of personal abilities and weaknesses, so the descriptive element of a clear self-image is crucial, the choice itself is programmatic, and it has to meet the existential need to feel worthwhile. The three key elements of identity formation are all present.

The Experience of Unemployment

Given the strong arguments made in the last section about the importance of employment to psychological well-being, it is not surprising that the effects

Table 4:   Job gains and losses in Britain, 1981–96

Job losses	
Mining and utilities	442 000
Minerals and metal products	435 000
Transport	357 000
Construction	307 000
Job Gains	
Computer related	916 000
Social work	450 000
Hotels and restaurants	334 000
Education	247 000

of unemployment have received considerable attention. Perhaps the first point to note is that it is not a uniform experience (Fryer and Ullah, 1987), those unemployed do not form a homogeneous group. One significant variable, that of gender, will be explored in the next section. For the moment the discussion will be centred on two age groups, and the effects of unemployment on youth and on adults.

In the years 1945–80 there was little widespread unemployment in Britain. Since then there have been two recessions which have raised the general level, but has had a particularly adverse effect on the young, the unskilled and on males. The years since 1980 have seen a major restructuring of the labour market as *Table 4* reveals. The extent of instability in the market is reflected in the fact that in 1995 278 000 women and 484 000 men were made redundant.

The issue of youth unemployment has received considerable attention, for example by being a focus of the major ESRC-financed 16–19 Initiative (Banks and Evans, 1989, Roberts, Parsell and Connolly, 1989, and Roberts and Parsell, 1989). The expectation might have been that the absence of the socializing force of employment would produce considerable disturbance and alienation among the youth. In fact, the picture which emerged was more complicated.

In the short term, the young cope fairly well as not all the strictures of unemployment affected them. There was no loss in earnings and hence no decline in the standard of living. There was no loss of status, in fact, they enjoyed a higher status than their peers who were still in school. Because a whole cohort of youngsters were suffering from the same experience they were able to set up informal social and support groups among themselves. The experience was shared with others so it was less traumatic. In essence, the period provided an extended moratorium for them. In the longer term, however, the balance could move to a less favourable position, as the youth could lose confidence in their abilities, lose habits of work and punctuality, and develop a growing resentment at living on a small income. Winefield *et al.* (1993) describe the eventual effects of unemployment on young people, such as depression, anomie and loss of self-esteem.

Unemployment among adults who have previously enjoyed regular work proves far more immediately damaging (e.g. Fryer and Ullah, 1987 and Super, 1957). They have already made the psychological investment in a career and now they discover that the investment has not paid. They experience both a loss of status and a reduction in earnings. The whole life-style, the rhythm of living in going to work at certain times, is broken. Their friends may still be working so there does not exist at hand a support group with whom one can spend the day. Even conventional retirement from employment, which is long-anticipated and is an experience shared by others, can be an unpleasant experience. Early redundancy can be traumatic.

The significance of these comments in terms of the identity model is that they demonstrate that identity is not solely an issue of adolescence. Unemployment provides a threat to identity which can be even more damaging to the adult than the adolescent. We must distinguish between this involuntary experience of mid-life unemployment and may well represent an escape from a previous foreclosed position.

Although paid employment is still a dominant component in shaping identity the general increase in wealth has made issues of leisure interests and material consumption assume a larger role. This consideration, alongside the rapid and immense changes in employment patterns, suggest that it may be unwise for a person to invest too much of their psychological well-being into their vocational identity. At the very least youth may need to anticipate the possibility of career changes occurring during adulthood. In this event, how does the individual retain a sense of personal continuity, hence of integrity? Possibly the existential component of identity may have to assume a more major role to meet this need. In this event, there are major implications for the young, particularly those males who rely on occupational choice to shape their identity.

Gender and Career

Traditionally, there have been two distinct ways in which work has been gendered. Globally, there has been the greater salience of work in the psychological development of males. More specifically, particular types of work have been perceived as more appropriate for one gender or the other.

Employment has played different roles within the life of men and women. The men have been the main earners, hence their work was vital in financing the family. Women have had to combine outside work with the duties involved in caring for the family so that a personal career tended to be subordinated to these other demands. Societal expectations are different, as Hutt (1979) pointed out, 'What is to be deplored . . . is the value system which depreciates the attributes and work of women, so that women underestimate their ability' (p. 193). What is not clear is the extent these gender divisions still persist. Clearly, a variety of changes, ranging from the effects of Equal Opportunities legislation through to the contemporary demands of the labour market for skilled personnel, have blunted the differences. Females now fill half the student places in higher education, so to that extent the gender differences have vanished. Certainly overt discrimination has largely disappeared, and an able girl is as likely to succeed as a boy, especially if she receives support from the family, but at some levels the differences are still apparent.

The author has found that when fourteen-year-old school pupils are asked to complete the sentence 'In ten years time I . . .' about two thirds of the boys refer to a career in completing the sentence. The remaining third give a variety of responses, ranging from references to being married to flippant replies about being dead or in prison. By contrast, over half the girls refer to marriage and motherhood and a quarter mention their career. A few mention both. Such data, obtained from several hundred British school pupils, indicates important differences in the adolescent anticipation of adulthood, and the importance of employment within it. So although the most able girls can compete on equal terms, the slightly less able girls see paid employment as a secondary factor in their identity development.

Experience of school teaching shows that boys are still subjected to greater family pressure to choose a career which is likely to be permanent, well paid and of high status. Girls receive less help, and less pressure to choose, and often they will only make a decision when the need arises, and then they will be more strongly influenced by their peers. Parents will still accept their daughter going into poorly paid work, arguing 'as long as she is happy . . . it may not be forever'.

Such differences in societal pressures can be seen by contrasting the story of *The Prime of Miss Jean Brodie* with *The Dead Poets Society*. Both stories tell of a charismatic, unorthodox teacher working within a conventional and conservative school. In both cases this teacher attracts a cult following from some of the pupils but is viewed with suspicion, or even hostility, by other teachers. But there are gender differences. The former story tells of a female teacher in a girls' school, and here the main concern is that the girls may be tempted into precocious sexual activity. The latter story tells of a male teacher in a boys' school, and the concern is that the boys become seduced from conventional careers, such as law, into the unconventional, such as acting. In both cases the teacher is touching on the primary concern of parents with regard to their adolescent offspring.

There is a further social pressure acting on boys which originates from the peer group. We have seen that boys tend to be very competitive and are constantly challenging each other to establish a hierarchy of power. In school this competition is fought out in two main ways, initially in athletics or on the games field, later in the classroom as well. Sporting success often gives a boy high esteem among his peers. High academic ability may win some more muted respect. This competitiveness continues after school but through different means, particularly the possession of a well-paid and high status job and the obvious and visible signs, such as the company car, which success brings. In these ways the old system of competition being canalized to some socially acceptable end, leading to the creation of social hierarchies, is maintained in the world of work. It could be argued that the entrepreneurial success of a capitalist society is based on the carrying over of male adolescent competitiveness to the world of work. As noted earlier, within the female peer group competition is less strong, discourse is framed so that the participants provide support for each other. In this social context competition to enter the world of work seems less relevant.

Given these different social pressures acting on boys and girls we might postulate differences in identity development. From a study of over 3000 American adolescents Douvan and Adelson (1966) suggested 'Boys tend to construct identity around vocational choice; in most cases girls do not. For most boys the question of "what to be" begins with work and the job, and he is likely to define himself and to be identified by occupation' (p. 17). But they go on to warn that '. . . there is more to total identity than occupation', and suggest that males tend to ignore other identity needs at this stage of their life. By contrast, 'Girls clearly invest less in an image of their future work than boys do. They have a less differentiated image of their future work, a less discriminating view of the content of the particular job to which they aspire' (p. 36).

This view is shared by Marcia (1980), 'The predominant concerns of most girls are not with occupation and ideology. Rather, they are concerned with the establishment and maintenance of personal relationships' (p. 179). He points out that when a girl does try to assert herself by placing the first priority on her career she may fail to gain the support from parents and teachers that a boy would receive. Consequently, the reaction of others tends to challenge her emerging sense of identity, whereas a boy would likely to receive confirmation. Under these conditions it is not surprising that girls often settle for a 'pseudo exploration' of career possibilities (Osipow, 1975).

Further evidence comes from Hodgson and Fisher (1979) who in a study of occupational identity of college students found that the males often had reached the identity attainment status while the females were more frequently foreclosed or even at the diffuse stage. Matteson (1975) showed that with Danish youth the males had given more attention to the alternative occupations on offer than the females. Such findings should cause no surprise, they are what we might anticipate, but they have been seen to advance the idea that females are naturally more foreclosed than males. However, this evidence, drawn from the study of the vocational aspect of identity, that females tend to foreclose more has to be balanced against that relating to sexuality, where it is the males that foreclose.

One further gender difference can be noted. The males tend to be more single minded in investing so much of their hopes for the future in their occupational choice. This singleness of purpose can makes choices simpler, but can carry some penalties. When things do not work out, for example through redundancy, then the danger is that the male is completely devastated, having no other sources of self-esteem to call on. Females face a more difficult choice earlier on in attempting to cope with career and home commitments, but as their emotional investment has been split they can manage better if one element proves disappointing. Faced with redundancy the female may be able to persuade herself that her career was always subordinate to that of her husband and also to the domestic demands made on her, so the setback can be taken more calmly. More pertinently to adolescents, the initial difficulty in gaining employment will tend to be more damaging for young men, and we saw in Chapter 1 that it is among this group that unemployment is highest.

Identity and a Career in Science

Much of the discussion in this chapter has been in terms of generalities, it might therefore prove illuminating to examine one career option in some detail, as a case study, in order to see how the model of identity works out in a specific context. I have chosen the example of science for two reasons: that it has been researched more fully than many other professions, and it displays a strong gender differential.

Although females make up half of our undergraduates within that overall figure lurk some major differentials. Women are in a majority in some subjects, including most language based areas, but only fill about 16 per cent of the physics places and 13 per cent of the engineering and technology places. This shortfall of females in the physical sciences and technology has received considerable attention both nationally (e.g. Kelly, 1987 and Harding, 1986) and internationally, for example, in the reports of the international Gender and Science and Technology (GASAT) organization.

Many of the explanations offered for the discrepancy have reiterated the biological determinist position, and time and time again the arguments have not stood up to scrutiny. There is some evidence, albeit not clear-cut, that girls perform better than boys at tests of verbal skills, but do slightly less well at tests of mathematical and spatial skills (Maccoby and Jacklin, 1975). At first sight this finding may appear to offer the explanation for subject differentials, but a more detailed examination of the data raises doubts. These reported differences in cognitive abilities are very small, usually only of the magnitude of 0.2 standard mean difference, and only the large sample sizes have allowed such differences to emerge as statistically significant. In crude terms this data may mean that for every one hundred boys with the ability to pursue a career in science and technology there will only be a pool of eighty or ninety girls. It can be seen that the ratio obtained from such figures is very different from those actually found among undergraduates. On the basis of every known test of ability there are not only enough females in our population to take their half share of the jobs in science and technology, but, in fact, enough to fill every single post in these fields. If females are so deficient in spatial skills, and that area shows the biggest differential, then why is it the majority of students in art and design courses are women?

Ironically, within science we find the topic which has long attracted many women is that of crystallography, a specialism which must be the most demanding of spatial abilities.

One current manifestation of biological determinism is that of brain hemisphere dominance. The argument is advanced that men and women possess different dominant hemispheres, as research shows that the left hemisphere is responsible for verbal activities. Women tend to possess greater verbal abilities so, it is argued, they must be more left hemisphere dominant. But the left hemisphere is also the centre for logical sequential thought in contrast to the more intuitive and holistic right hemisphere. In this case, we arrive at the contradictory belief that women must be more right hemisphere dominant. In fact, the only gender difference which can be sustained is that women have less lateralized brains. In other words the two hemispheres can overlap more in their activity, which might express itself in a more holistic mode of thinking. There is nothing here to explain the absence of women from science.

If we shift our attention to the process of career and subject choice among school pupils then some interesting results emerge. Presumably, the young people have to match their perceptions of careers against their self-image to see what is compatible. What images do such students have of science? This field has been fully researched (Gardner, 1975, Schibeci, 1984) and a clear picture emerges. Scientists are seen to be rather conservative, emotionally reticent males, more interested in things than other people. They are seen to be concerned with abstract, remote issues, things which are not relevant to everyday life and the general population. The really important point is that this perception is shared equally by boys and girls, by those who opt for science and those who do not. In this event, different subject choices do not arise from *different perceptions*, but must come from *different valuations* placed on such perceptions when matched with the self-image.

Choosing a career in science and technology is very different for the young female than for the young male. The latter makes an easy and obvious choice. He enters a male-dominated field, one which will tend to attract approval from adults and peers and confirms his masculinity. The girl has to make a more difficult choice. She has to do something which is somewhat unconventional and be willing to work in situations in which females are in a small minority. Such a choice requires some commitment and determination.

We can now relate the career choices to Marcia's identity statuses. Neither boys nor girls in the moratorium status are likely to be attracted to science as it is usually perceived. Young people experiencing moratorium may be worried about many issues, the existence of God, politics, the risk of nuclear warfare, green issues, or their own sexuality and ability to cope as adults. The instrumental values of science appear not to address such issues, and thus have limited relevance.

A number of males and females who have reached the identity achievement status will opt for careers in science and technology. As these people have made a considered choice, weighing up the alternatives and recognizing their own strengths and limitations, the decisions are likely to lead to career success.

When we move on to the people who are foreclosing a big gender difference emerges. Girls who foreclose on their career will opt for something with feminine image and where they can work with their friends. Science does not meet that need. Boys experiencing foreclosure will choose something which does not challenge their fragile masculinity, and science is a possible choice. The fact that science appears to be more concerned with things than people enhances its appeal. Maslow (1966) pointed out that the image of the unemotional scientist had much in common with that of the Hollywood cowboy, and both appeal to the insecure boy.

> . . . look at the acting out and the fantasy elements in the cowboy figure . . . The most obvious characteristics of the boy's dream of glory are there. He is fearless, he is strong, he is 'lone' . . . Apart from his horse he doesn't love anyone, or at least he doesn't express it except in the most understated, implied, reverse-English way . . . He is in every respect imaginable the far, polar opposite of the pansy type of homosexual in whose realm he includes all the arts, all of culture . . . (p. 37)

If this link between identity and a science career is correct then we can anticipate certain outcomes. As the girls who opt for science only come from the identity achievement group, while the boys come from both the achievement and the foreclosure groups, we can predict both quantitative and qualitative differences between males and females choosing science. The males come from a much larger cohort, so we would expect there to be many more males entering science, which accords with the evidence. We would also expect many males choosing science to display typical foreclosure characteristics, essentially avoiding anything which might force them to abandon the false maturity and security of foreclosure. When we look at the evidence of the personality characteristics of male scientists we find just the features we anticipate. The men will tend to be conservative, authoritarian and reticent about emotional issues (Head, 1979 and 1985). The evidence is overwhelming.

> The young scientist often reaches maturity after a lopsided early develop-ment . . . If success rewards his consolatory scholarly efforts during adoles-cence, he may in later years tend to cultivate intellectual activity exclusively. In this way absorption in the intellectual life will be paralleled by an increasing withdrawal from athletic and social and psychosexual activities. (Kubie, 1954, p. 112)

Or, '. . . The interviews reveal that scientists are not able to give the most significant part of themselves to home and family . . .' (Eiduson, 1962, p. 50). The logical structure of science, its apparent sense of order, would appeal to the authoritarian personality.

Does it matter that there is such a gender bias in the uptake of careers in science and technology? There are three conceptually different reasons for answering in the affirmative. First, is the argument about equal opportunities, that women should be well represented in all walks of life, including professional science. Secondly, there is the point about the widespread shortage of skilled personnel in these fields and women represent the largest pool of untapped talent. Finally, there is the argument that the highjack of science, not just by males, but particularly foreclosed males, contributes to the common unease about the role and use of science. One of the concerns about contemporary scientists is that they too readily give their talents to inhumane ends, such as the production of weapons of war, the infliction of pain on animals or the spoiling of the natural environment. Such simple criticisms applied to complex issues are, of course, unfair, but in so far they have a basis of reality these would arise from the strong male foreclosure values found in science.

If we want to make science and technology more accountable and more caring then we need to attract more people from outside the foreclosure status. One tactic would be to delay subject and career choice until later in adolescence when such choices will be less frequently made through foreclosure and more by those who have gained a firm identity. There is extensive survey evidence that university students in the humanities and social science show an increasing enthusiasm for their subject as their studies progress but, within the natural sciences and technology, there is widespread boredom and disillusionment which increases with time. Probably one factor contributing to this apparent loss of interest is that many of the male science students made their initial career choice through the process of foreclosure and then later, as they matured, they regretted that choice. Delaying choice until the students are more mature could therefore reduce the distress which is likely to accompany the recognition that one has made a mistake.

Above all, we would want to attract more women, in the hope that they could bring the feminine qualities of caring and concern more into the arena of science. This change cannot be brought about by presenting a different science curriculum for girls, for this would certainly be seen as second best and would disadvantage the girls, but in the way school science is set into the human context, so that its social value and relevance is stressed. Intervention studies to promote 'girl friendly' physics in this fashion show that it is possible to bring about both qualitative and quantitative changes in the uptake by girls of such subjects (Head and Ramsden, 1990). The quantitative change was manifest in the fact that more girls opted to specialize in science. Prior to the intervention most of the girls who chose science came from a narrow range of Psychological Types, as measured by the Myers-Briggs Type Inventory, but the intervention brought about a qualitative change, with those opting for science now coming from a wide range of personality types. Identity theory allows us to describe the dynamics of subject and career choice and plan effective intervention.

Identity and Vocational Guidance

Only relatively recently has attention been drawn, for example by Raskin (1985 and 1989), to the problem that identity theorists and vocational guidance professionals have been working without any communication or cooperation with each other, despite being interested in similar issues and the same population. Already from the evidence discussed in this chapter some implications of identity theory should be apparent. Vondracek *et al.* (1995) have related indecision about careers to identity status among adolescent students, with the achievement students showing less indecision, as might be expected, but with foreclosure students seeming to be less secure than we might have anticipated.

Perhaps the most obvious point is that career choice, like most crucial life choices, is not solely a cognitive act. What people feel may be as important as what they think. Likewise, temperament may be as important to happiness in a given profession as cognitive abilities. Too often vocational guidance is centred simply on cognitive abilities, and if there is a match between the person and the job then all is well. But for a successful outcome to identity achievement the young person has to make a series of choices which end up yielding a consistent and coherent set of objectives. Unless this need to relate vocational choice to the other aspects of identity is recognized there are dangers. They may become disillusioned with their career or prove incapable of identifying a life-style which allows effective functioning of the whole person.

Career choice has many implications, ranging from expectations of financial return to the constraints placed on one's behaviour once in post. Someone who is temperamentally unconformist in outlook and behaviour would be well steered away from a post which demands conformity in dress and behaviour. Alongside questions of abilities go those of desired life-style. What do you want to do when not at work? Where do you want to live? Does travel away from home excite or appal you? Will the demands of this job cut across your preferences for your life-style, including your sexual and emotional relationships? From where do you gain a sense of worthwhileness, of self-esteem in your life? From asking such questions of themselves young people are helped to make a mature and sensible choice, one which allows them to develop all the various aspects of themselves.

It is notoriously difficult to predict changes in employment patterns. For example, I have on file several articles written ten or twenty years ago predicting that the new technology would cause us all to be working half-time in ten or twenty years' time. The reality has proved to be the exact reverse. Where the technological revolution has been most influential, for example in the stock exchange or banking, working hours have drastically increased. The portable telephone has become the symbol of our times, the totem of the executive workaholic. But despite that cautionary note, we can safely make some predictions.

The demands of employment are going to change more rapidly. This acceleration of change is already with us. We have already experienced the loss of jobs in fields such as mining and manufacturing and parallel changes can be predicted in fields such as banking. With new generations of computers rapidly replacing each other, the person who is competent one year may be a computer illiterate the next. Yesterday's skills have little market value. What this means for the young person is that their occupational choice may not serve them for life. They have to make a commitment, for without that nothing is achieved, but be open to reconsider at a later date. In terms of identity development this underlines the danger of foreclosing on a career, for inflexibility is inherent to foreclosure.

It will be wise to discourage early specialization in school. Delay gives the adolescent time to mature and be able to achieve a genuine identity. Furthermore, the extended provision of a broad, general education keeps the options open until later. In turn, this delay will affect the dynamics of adolescent development. As we have already noted, occupational choice is often the first element of identity which is resolved, particularly with boys. If they are forced to maintain a moratorium in relation to occupation then they may have to confront issues of sexuality and ideology without having the security of part of their identity being resolved.

There are implications here for counselling and social education in schools. With the decline in the role of employment in socializing adolescents into adulthood issues of sexuality and ideology may need to be addressed more effectively than has been common hitherto. Previously, many adolescents, particularly males, gained their first firm sense of identity through the making and realization of career choices, but that possibility is becoming more difficult. Young people may need to anchor their identity in their social and emotional life while occupational choice is still unresolved.

Activity

If you are working with adolescents in any capacity plan a vocational guidance scheme. It should recognize the following points. Career choice depends on matching self against the demands of the job. Are the youngsters fully informed about the latter — the entry requirements, the drawbacks and benefits of such work and its potentialities? Have they adequate self knowledge? Obviously they can learn something from their school grades and reports and a variety of informal comments, from friends, family and teachers, but is this adequate? Marcia's model indicates that their choice should involve commitment. Have the adolescents just drifted into a career choice or are they committed? Secondly, the choice should be their own, not something imposed on them by others. Is there evidence of personal thought and choice, as distinct from foreclosure?

Chapter Summary

- effective career choice comes from both affective and cognitive concerns, deep rooted in the psychology of the individual;
- serendipity can provide a trigger for a previously inarticulated desires to surface, it does not in itself cause the desire;
- for many adolescents vocational choice represents the first public declaration of their individuality;
- career choice is strongly gendered, both because various jobs are seen to be more appropriate for one gender, and because a career is seen to be more salient to male psychological development;
- current high levels of youth unemployment can be damaging for those involved, although in the short term the young are surprisingly resilient;
- with such unemployment prevailing, adolescents will have to rely on other aspects of their life more to help gain their sense of identity;
- vocational guidance will become increasingly more crucial, not least in preparing the young to be flexible in entering a rapidly changing labour market.

Further Reading

BANKS, M., BATES, I., BREAKWELL, G., BYNNER, J., EMLER, N., JAMIESON, L. and ROBERTS, K. (1992) *Careers and Identities*, Milton Keynes: Open University Press. This book contains the report of the major ESRC research initiative of 16 to 19-year-olds in four areas of Britain.

WILLIS, P. (1977) *Learning to Labour; How Working Class Kids Get Working Class Jobs*, Aldershot: Gower. The labour market has changed since he wrote this book, but he describes the underlying dynamics which go a long way to explain the current problems facing young men.

WINEFIELD, A.H., TIGGEMANN, M., WINEFIELD, H.R. and GOLDNEY, R.D. (1993) *Growing Up With Unemployment; A Longitudinal Study of its Psychological Impact*, London: Routledge. A useful book, my only reservation is that it is based on Australian experience, which may differ from that in Britain.

Chapter 7

Beliefs and Values

The challenge of achieving an identity was encapsulated for youth in Classical Greece by the question, 'How shall we live?', a question needing to be answered at two levels. In part, it is programmatic, asking a question about what one is going to do in the future. But is also asking about beliefs and values, by what principles or standards will one live. The two connect, of course, because from beliefs a moral code may be derived, which in turn affects behaviour. We can recall another Classical saying, 'We choose our destiny by our choice of Gods.'

The last two chapters, relating to sexuality and occupational identity, have dealt almost solely with the practical issues of living. In this chapter we continue with the theme of planning the practical aspects of life, particularly in respect to those aspects beyond career and social relationships, expressed through a variety of choices generating what we might call a life-style. At the same time, we are encountering the existential need to feel that our life is meaningful, and for many this need is met by subscribing to an ideology. The requirement that life should be seen to be meaningful, and the role of things bigger than oneself, enshrined in myths and religions, seem to be a fundamental human need. Looking back to commentaries written about 1920, I have in mind the Bloomsbury Group writers, philosophers like Bertrand Russell, and the political commentators hailing the Russian Revolution of 1917. We find a widespread view that religious belief was rapidly fading away and would finally disappear from the world by the end of the century. The contrast between such prophecy and the reality gives cause for thought. A theological argument might be that divine will has intervened, although a cynic noticing that the loss in conventional church membership has been compensated for by a growth in New Age cults and charismatic preachers might recall Chesterton's words that those who believe in nothing end up in believing anything. To the psychologist the lesson is that the need to believe is very deep rooted in the psyche, whatever the cause may be. For this reason we can appreciate why ideology was identified as the third main arena in which identity can develop.

I must confess to disliking Erikson's term 'ideology'. The possession of an ideology suggests that the person is able to articulate and justify a coherent philosophy. Many people would find that task daunting, and may therefore be unfairly dismissed as having failed to move beyond a diffusion state with regard to this identity component. But the articulation of abstract and general principles is a challenging task for one who is not used to such discussion. Most people, however, will reveal an implicit value-system if asked questions about concrete instances. From the initially discrete set of responses one will probably detect a pattern revealing an underlying set of coherent beliefs. In fact, if someone readily articulates an ideological position we might suspect that they have foreclosed, and are simply repeating something learned complete from an other. For this reason I prefer to talk about the less pre-emptive terms of *beliefs* and *values.*

There is certainly evidence that in adolescence these issues come to the fore. The most likely age for a sudden religious conversion is sixteen, and many adolescents experience a moratorium in which they display sudden enthusiasms for idealistic causes. Issues such as nuclear disarmament or Green issues will be hotly debated. It is not coincidental that some political extreme groups have targeted their recruitment drives on teenagers, for example those attending football matches. These moods tend to be labile, with the adolescent switching rapidly from apparent commitment to cynicism and back again, before settling on a personal set of values.

Parker (1985) provides a succinct summary of the considerable body of work relating to religious conversion among the young. He suggests that there is a distinction to be made between those for whom conversion is the culmination of a long-drawn process, for whom the religious experience represents identity achievement, and those who undergo an abrupt and un-expected conversion, who undergo foreclosure. People in the latter group are likely to be motivated by emotional, rather than intellectual or religious considerations, having been unhappy and alienated prior to the religious experience. In the short-term, the experience reduces anxiety, as decisions are made for the individual who tends to be shielded from external demands and distractions which might cause them to question their new faith. In the longer term, there seems to be widespread disillusionment among those who experienced sudden conversion, with apostasy or defection levels as high as 90 per cent, probably because the individual finds the emotional needs are still not met. This high level of defection motivates some religious groups to cause their members to live in self-contained social groups, in which strong peer support can be given to members and at the same time external influences can be minimized, so that defection is obstructed.

Adams (1985) gives a parallel description of identity and political social-ization. The achievement of a political sense of identity both helps the individual develop a set of values to handle practical living and, at the same time, serves to socialize the adolescent into the social institutions and value systems of the culture. Occasionally emotional needs precipitate a response like that of religious conversion but generally the decisions are more founded on cognitive and social considerations. The choice therefore is likely to be less sudden and less fickle.

Erikson and the Psychoanalytic Tradition

Blos (1962) described adolescence as involving a 'second individuation process'. He argued that by about the age of three the child has learnt to internalize the moral code of the parents, so when separated from the parents the child is still able to judge what the parent would rule in a particular circumstance, and be able to follow this ruling. The adolescent finds this internalized parental code is not adequate to meet the new demands being placed on the self, for example in coping with the emerging sense of sexuality, so this code has to be replaced. The move from this early foreclosed position to a moratorium, in which a new code is worked out for oneself, is the process Blos described as individuation.

Erikson introduced two further elements into the argument. The first idea was the social role of an ideology,

> For it is through their ideology that social systems enter into the fiber of the next generation and attempt to absorb into their lifeblood the rejuvenative power of youth. Adolescence is thus a vital regenerator in the process of social evolution, for youth can offer its loyalties and energies both to the conservation of that which continues to feel true and to the revolutionary correction of that which has lost its regenerative significance. (Erikson, 1968, p. 134)

This statement addressed his concern that there should be balance between change and continuity, and that a sure identity could only be developed if the adolescent recognized and respected the cultural traditions, so that the personal dynamic worked symbiotically with the social dynamic. In his view the adoption of an ideology avoided the misery of social anarchy, which might arise if the young were completely out of sympathy with the prevailing order, or if they introduced too many traumatic changes when they assumed power. For Erikson the ideology espoused in political and religious systems provided a mechanism for ensuring a degree of continuity within society.

Erikson's second point was that an ideology served an individual by being an organizer of experience, which in turn, provides an anticipation of new experiences. We can make an analogy between this idea and that of concept development in children. For the very young child almost every experience is novel, and hence nothing can be anticipated. However, the child has the capacity to learn. Experiences will be placed into categories, so that the child does not have to meet every situation as a novelty, but is able to anticipate certain things will be pleasurable, and others not, because they share features with similar things previously experienced. Eventually, we are able to live our lives largely through vicarious experience, we do not have to actually undergo every pain and tribulation to imagine what they might be like. Our ability to organize experience, recognize categories, and anticipate outcomes, allows us to proceed more effectively and comfortably through life. These concepts and categories learnt in childhood refer to concrete things, but adolescence is the time when attention shifts to the world of abstract ideas. Without some organizing system, or ideology, Erikson argued, every situation will pose a moral dilemma such that the adolescent can only react slowly while working out an appropriate response. A coherent belief system serves the adolescent by allowing an almost instant response to moral dilemmas. Only if they are armed with this ideological tool will adolescents be able to function effectively in the adult world. We might note a similarity with Adler's argument that people need a 'guiding fiction' to live by, and that this anticipation of the future may shape behaviour as potently as memories of the past. Adler's use of the word fiction is meant to indicate that it is something constructed by the individual, it is not meant to imply that it is necessarily false.

Finally, Erikson (1968) reminds us of the importance of ideological identity and the stark consequences of malfunctioning in this arena, 'for when established identities become outworn and while new ones remain vulnerable, special crises compel men to wage holy wars, by the cruelest means, against those who seem to question or threaten their as yet unsafe ideological bases' (p. 191). Although in many of his writings he seem to show a degree of social conservatism, in the sense that he emphasizes the need for the young to adjust to their society, it is clear from the passage quoted that he also recognized the danger of a society which failed to adjust to changing circumstances.

Diversity and Culture

Much of the work on ideology and identity has been carried out in the United States and Canada and research on the ideological component of identity has been commonly explored by asking about allegiance to churches and political parties. With students in these countries a spread among the four identity statuses is found. With British students we find much weaker allegiances, with the majority expressing no strong views on religious or political matters, and indicating that they have given little thought to these matters. In terms of identity theory they give little evidence of either commitment or exploration. One possible explanation is that young people in Britain are less mature than their American counterparts, but this finding does not extend to other aspects of identity, such as career and personal relationships. It is more likely that we are picking up on our cultural difference, the extent to which young people enter the discourse of religion and politics.

A much higher proportion of the population in the United States regularly attend church than in Britain. Despite widespread cynicism about politicians I think Americans are more likely to believe in the importance of politics, if only because American leaders wield immense power on a global scale.

Table 5:   *Percentage of British youth expressing strong views on different issues*

	%
Race	37
Roles of men and women	34
Sex	30
Environment	26
Youth Training	23
Education	22
Taxation, government services and spending	21
Police, rules, law and authority	19
Family	18
Regional Contrasts	17
Political parties, processes and politicians	16

Source: BANKS, M. *et al.* (1992) *Careers and Identities*, Milton Keynes: Open University Press.

More commonly among British youth we encounter the statement that we are an insignificant country with little power to determine our fate and it does not matter who is in government.

Alongside these differences in beliefs about the salience of religion and politics there are differences in the rhetoric of national populations. Here I will make another comparison, between Britain and Poland. In the 1980s the latter country was on the boundary of two competing systems, which could be described in terms of competition between the two super-powers of Russia and the United States; or a clash between the two economic systems of capitalism and state control; or could be expressed in two rival ideologies of Roman Catholicism and Marxism. Whatever the choices peoples might have made, and regardless of the reasons for their choice, they were able to describe an ideological decision. The population had been extensively exposed to the rhetoric of the conflicting ideological systems. I can give one personal account of the differences in ideological systems. When lecturing in China I was taken back by the opening question 'Is it possible to make science compatible with dialectical materialism?'. As I gasped for breath it dawned on me that I was being asked to comment on the Cultural Revolution, which they had recently experienced, when scientists were removed from the universities and made to labour in the fields and factories. The justification for this action had been that none should not be isolated in academic seclusion but that everyone should work alongside the mass of the population. As no one I know in Britain has had this experience no one has ever posed such a question.

There is another difficulty of research in this field; that the form of the question dictates the response. Asked about religion and politics British youth appear to be ill educated or immature, but this finding does not deny that they hold a set of strongly felt beliefs. Banks *et al.* (1992), in their survey report of British youth in four regions, identified the issues about which the youth expressed strong views, as shown in *Table 5*.

Clearly in the British context formal political allegiances attract less interest than issues of equal opportunities and care of the environment. Our youth may be said to care about issues but tend not to express their beliefs in the form of a sophisticated ideological statement.

We must also avoid the danger of simply judging one population, that of teenagers, solely by criteria which have evolved in a different population. Adults may see contemporary adolescents as being without morals, citing greater tolerance with respect to a range of sexual behaviours and a lack of deference to authority as evidence. But in some ways, for example, with respect to the care of the environment, young people tend to display a greater moral awareness and commitment.

Gender and Moral Development

One of the most extensively researched aspects, and one which has attracted much controversy in recent years, has been that of moral development. But before looking at the details we might like to consider the notion of moral development. The very form of the words involves the assumption that there is something which develops. This model would be in accord with the idea of Original Sin, in which children have to be initiated into a society governed by moral precepts. There has been a counter proposition, of Original Virtue, voiced in the opening words of Rousseau's *Emile*, 'God makes all things good; man meddles with them and they become evil'. The latter stance has been reflected in the twentieth century in the work of A.S. Neill at Summerfield and in the de-schooling writing, such as by Holt and Illich, which will be discussed in the next chapter.

Which story should we believe? There is ample evidence of confusion. For example, in the nineteenth century British Public School masters subscribed to a Christian philosophy but often adopted a *laissez faire* attitude to the management of boarding houses, in the belief that the goodness within the boys would prevail. In the event, bullying and sadism too often prevailed. It was precisely this situation which Arnold of Rugby School felt bound to challenge. It is probably an error to reduce the understanding of complex situations to choosing one or other of two simple propositions, but if forced I have to confess that I fear that Golding's *Lord of the Flies* was close to the truth. Young people do behave badly too often unless made to face ethical questions about the consequences of their actions. To this extent the concept of moral development has some validity.

Piaget (1932), in a study of moral development, used his usual technique of asking individuals to talk through how they would solve a problem, but did not follow up this early work, it being left to Lawrence Kohlberg to pursue the task. In this section, I want to explore the contrast between two workers concerned with moral development, Kohlberg and Carol Gilligan. The latter postulates a gender bias in the work of the former and this debate sheds light on some aspects of adolescent development. Neither worker directly addressed issues of identity, although the connections can be easily made.

Kohlberg developed a cognitive-developmental perspective to make sense of many aspects of psychological development. For example, he suggested that gender differences arose principally from learnt behaviour. Kohlberg (for example, 1981) applied this model to moral development. He accepted Piaget's description of cognitive development, that the child progresses through an invariant hierarchy of qualitatively different modes of thinking, and produced a parallel hierarchy for moral attitudes. He believed that a higher level of cognitive development was necessary, but not sufficient, to exercise higher levels of moral judgment.

His research methodology was to pose a problem or dilemma which did not offer an easy solution and ask the respondent what one should do in this situation. For example, would it be right for someone to steal money in order to buy medicine for one of the family who is ill? Or, should one tell one's parents if a sibling had done something dishonest? He placed the responses into six stages within three levels.

Preconventional level

This is marked by a simple concern for the self interest. People and situations will be judged to be good or not according to the criterion that the respondent is likely to receive benefits and avoid penalties. Stage 1, the least mature, is shown by responses indicating simply an attempt to avoid punishment. Stage 2 is characterized by taking actions which positively benefit oneself, regardless of the consequences for others.

Conventional level

The main concern is to be popular, to win approval from others and avoid criticism and censure. It can be seen that even at this second level the ultimate motive is selfishness, but it is an indirect selfishness, one which might accept a degree of giving in order to win approval from others by conforming to shared values. Stage 3 is shown by simple conformity to the norms of the social group, while at Stage 4 respondents have a keen sense of a social system which brings order to our society.

Postconventional or principled level

At this level the subject can distance his or her immediate needs from moral judgments. Actions will be judged in the light of some general principles, and there will be a measure of self-censorship to check that one is living up to these ideals. At Stage 5 the emphasis is on the importance of mutually agreed standards which benefit all, while at Stage 6 beliefs are articulated in terms of universal ethical principles.

Kohlberg's taxonomy attracted considerable attention and some criticism, for example that he only addressed some features of moral judgments

and failed to explain the content. The critics were slower to detect one crucial limitation of his model, that the original work had been conducted by
interviewing eighty-four boys aged ten to sixteen. When Kohlberg's tests
were carried out with girls they seemed to cluster at the conventional level
and very few reached the principled level. This difference was then commonly attributed to some deficiency in females which, it was argued, had
not been more widely appreciated as so many women only acted out their
moral judgments in the restricted domestic environment and did not need
to participate in the wider world of business and the professions.

Early on it was apparent that other studies, employing different methodologies, led to different findings from Kohlberg. For example, Bull (1969)
reported one survey which showed:

> Girls were found to be in advance of boys in their moral judgements in
> every area examined . . . Boys excel in the concrete situation, girls in the
> subtleties, both good and bad, of personal relationships. Girls are mainly
> concerned with the psychological and personal, boys with the physical . . . If
> concern for others is the heart of all morality, as indeed must be, the female
> is inherently more truly moral than the male. (pp. 42–3)

Despite this accumulation of contradictory evidence Kohlberg's work
remained the accepted canon until Gilligan (1982 a and b) raised a feminist
challenge,

> I first became aware of this bias while teaching with Kohlberg at Harvard
> . . . I interviewed several of the female dropouts in depth . . . These women
> were experiencing moral conflicts that simply could not be understood within
> Kohlberg's framework. (Gilligan, 1982b, p. 68)

Implicit in Kohlberg's thought was Freud's notion that moral sense
developed when the adolescent overcame the Oedipal conflict and emerged
with a strong super-ego. The Oedipal resolution is less clear-cut with girls so,
it was argued, they might possess a weaker super-ego to direct morality. In
fact, empirical evidence has never sustained this view. Gilligan argued, 'Psychological theories have fallen . . . into the same observational bias. Implicitly
adopting the male life as the norm, they have tried to fashion women out
of a masculine cloth' (Gilligan, 1982a, p. 6). She argued that moral development should be conceptualized as two different tasks for boys and girls.
For the former, the problem is to move from a selfish ego-centric view to
take account of others. For the latter, the task to contribute to the social
matrix and emerge with some measure of autonomy.

> While she places herself in relation to the world . . . he places the world in
> relationship to himself, as it defines his character, his position, and the qual-
> ity of his life. The contrast (is) between the self defined through separation
> and a self delineated through connection, between a self measured against

an abstract ideal of perfection and a self assessed through particular activities of care. (Gilligan, 1982a, p. 35)

What emerged from her study was the contrast between thinking and feeling, between objectivity and subjectivity, justice and mercy, between personal autonomy and care for others. Females tended to place greater weight on the second of each of these paired concerns. The males judge moral issues according to some abstract rules, females often invoke an element of empathy.

For example, if we show a film depicting a bar scene in which an argument leads on to a fight, then boys and girls will set different criteria to judge who was to blame. The boys will create a rule, that the first person to touch another, or the first person to use a weapon, was to blame, and hence they find the decision straightforward. Girls tend to puzzle about issues not made clear in the scene. Did the characters know each other? What had been their previous relationship? What motivated someone to say or do what they did? The boys will analyse the situation in order to identify the one specific thing which represents the breaking of the rules. The girls will tend to contextualize the scene in order to understand the total social dynamic in which the scene occurred.

The problem with Kohlberg's original tests is that they tended to draw the most mature responses from the boys but failed to do so for the girls. The boys saw the exercise as a game, which would have to be played by some implicit rules, and they set out to identify some such rule and play accordingly. The girls found it difficult to enter into the hypothetical situations which were presented to them, the exercise seemed unreal to them and did not stretch their imagination. The very methodology contained a gender bias.

Gilligan's work has been most influential for a number of reasons. First, because it was opportune. Feminist theory in the 1960s tended to deny the significance of gender differences. This attitude was understandable, for often differences in power, money and influence had been justified in terms of some supposed difference in mental or physical capacity. It was an obvious reaction to minimize the importance of such differences, and works which ran counter to this trend, e.g. Douvan and Adelson (1966) received a bad press. By the early 1980s the mood had changed. Feminist thought had moved on to accept the possibility of there being more significant gender differences than had been imagined earlier. The problem was now to identify and describe these differences, and Gilligan's work addressed that need. Nevertheless, it remains difficult to live with the notion of people being 'different but equal', for as soon as humans recognize differences they tend to attach values to them. Wherever people of different races or beliefs live together they are likely to enter competition leading to the more powerful oppressing the others.

A further appeal of Gilligan's model is that it coheres with so much other work on gender. It is easy to see how her description of the justice mode of thinking among males and the caring mode among females is a natural development from the differences experienced by young children, as described in Chapter 4, with the boys having to limit their competitiveness and aggression through the observance of rule-bound behaviour. Further links can be made. Lever (1976) made a study of play among children aged ten and eleven. She pointed out that dissent seems to have a different effect on boys and girls. Among the latter it seems to be damaging to the extent that the game has to be abandoned. Boys, however, play with a constant background of argument, which does not seem to inhibit the play but becomes part of it. Already the boys are showing the justice mode of thinking about disputes and rules and the girls being more concerned with personal relationships which are threatened by disputes.

Gilligan also allows us to reinterpret Horner's (1972) work on the fear of success which is sometimes found with females. Usually people are motivated to compete and succeed through the twin factors of the wish for success and fear of failure. Horner suggested that, in addition, some women have a fear of success and this quality has usually been attributed to a wish to be seen as feminine, rather than as competitive like men. Gilligan suggests that this feminine quality may not just be a wish to conform to a traditional sense of appropriate gender behaviour but from an active sense of what might be involved in being successful. Too often success for oneself can only be achieved through someone else experiencing failure and many women, Gilligan argues, would see in that event too high a price having to be paid for success. In other words, Gilligan's description of the different voice allows to describe many observed gender differences in a less pejorative way.

A few empirical studies in recent years have attempted to test Gilligan's theories in relation to identity development. For example, Mellor (1989) working with nearly four hundred adolescents related psychosocial development to the two main modes of self-definition, through separation from others and through connection with others. For those who defined self through separation from others males were the more psychosocially mature. For those who defined themselves in connection with others the females were the more mature, and in fact the most mature of the four sub-groups. Mellor commented that his findings 'lent support to the predictions that males and females use distinctive relational self-definitions to resolve specific crises. Data trends on measures of identity resolution for males and females with separate and connected self-definitions were consistent with Gilligan's view of gender differences in self–other relations' (p. 371).

What did Gilligan mean by the term a 'different voice'? Consider this passage:

> The tension between these perspectives is suggested by the fact that detachment, which is the mark of mature moral judgment in the justice perspective, becomes the moral problem in the care perspective, that is, the failure to attend to need. Conversely, attention to the particular needs and circumstances of

individuals, the mark of moral judgment in the care perspective, becomes the moral problem in the justice perspective, that is, failure to treat others fairly, as equals. (Gilligan and Attanucci, 1988, pp. 232–3)

The weak interpretation of her work would suggest that men and women have different priorities and, in dealing with moral issues, they tend to focus on different aspects of a situation, but otherwise the mental processes are very similar. In this event, effective communication can be established once the different priorities have been recognized. The strong interpretation is to adopt a stance of psycholinguistic relativity, arguing that men and women employ different languages which enshrine different concepts and values. In this case communication will inevitably be imperfect as each of us only has full access to one language code. Carol Gilligan has assured me that she intended the weaker version, that different people can overcome barriers and communicate effectively, provided that they take care to listen to each other. Nevertheless, her work is sometimes quoted as providing justification for the stronger interpretation and a radical stance with respect to gender differences.

One further outcome from her work is the realization that other assessment tools might contain a bias as the problems which she found with Kohlberg's tasks might occur more universally. There is ample evidence that girls tend to perform better in writing essays and boys in multiple choice tests. In part, the better verbal skills of girls may contribute to this difference, but increasingly it has become recognized that there are differences in thinking styles. Girls tend to dislike multiple choice tests for the same reasons that they dislike Kohlberg's tests, that they are being asked to make a firm decision on a basis of limited information. Boys recognize the exercise as a game with its own set of rules and attempt to win the game within these rules. The conclusion we can draw from this work is that most forms of testing have a gender bias and balance can only be obtained by employing a mix of methods. This finding is particularly ironical as multiple choice tests were initially proposed as an objective mode of testing. For further consideration of this topic *A Fair Test?* by Gipps and Murphy (1994) is recommended.

Foreclosure and Flexibility

As with all aspects of identity development, the adolescent acquisition of a sense of moral or ideological positioning in society depends on the twin processes of exploration and commitment. The former presents few problems. Facilitating thought among the young, is best done by asking them to consider possibilities and justify their conclusions. Teachers working within multi-faith schools have long learnt the tactics of this exercise, by looking at specific issues, such as abortion, the treatment of criminals and green issues, and inviting students to debate their stances on these matters.

The trickier problem is how, in this context, we deal with the need to develop a sense of commitment to a set of beliefs and values. Within a church school, or a committed family, there may seem to be no problem. Within a multi-cultural society accusations of indoctrination have to be recognized, and have some validity as commitment to varying beliefs can provide the basis for social instability — witness Northern Ireland. The question which, as a psychologist, interests me is how we can provide support without indoctrination. Possibly the key point is that commitment in isolation is dangerous, and is only likely to be helpful if reached after undergoing exploration. In other words, the crucial matter is to minimize foreclosure. At this stage, I want to make explicit and amplify a theme which has been developing, at least implicitly, in recent chapters; that of the relationship between the foreclosure status and certain other variables, such as learning.

Essentially a balance has to be struck between two demands. A person needs to possess a consistent set of values and beliefs if they are to operate effectively and achieve a mature identity. At the same time, they need to be flexible enough to change their mode of working when circumstances require such change. Those who are still at the identity diffusion stage, and those experiencing moratorium, may lack the desired degree of consistency, a quality common among adolescents. Inflexibility is characteristic of foreclosure. For such people we can rewrite Descartes' dictum 'I think, therefore I am' to 'I am what I think'. Their beliefs and values define the self, and revision of beliefs reached by foreclosure can threaten the sense of identity.

It has long been recognized that learning involves two processes which occur simultaneously: assimilation, that is the taking on of new ideas, and accommodation, that is the changing of the existing mental structure. The balance between these two processes will vary according to the task and the individual, but the overall effect of the new constructivist psychology has been to put increased emphasis on accommodation. Learning does not simply involve filling a vacuum with some new ideas, but requires former ideas to be modified, or even abandoned. The active mind causes people to anticipate formal teaching, so they develop their own informal ideas which may contradict what they experience in formal education. To take a trivial example, a child may believe that the sun goes round the earth, as common observation suggests this to be so, and this belief might block the learning the idea of the earth rotating around the sun.

Learning, the acquisition of a new ideas, involves in part the abandonment of prior ideas. If the individual has a strong emotional commitment to these prior ideas then learning may be resisted. The person who has foreclosed on his or her set of beliefs will be the least willing to change them. Foreclosure, therefore, imposes a mental rigidity which inhibits coping behaviour and learning. It represents the identity status most at risk in situations requiring mental change.

The penalty may have to be paid both by the individual and by a wider society. For the individual it is manifest in the inability to cope with change, such as that required in dealing with redundancy from work, or the inevitable changes accompanying ageing. For society it means that people who have managerial responsibility cannot adapt and learn so the whole enterprise suffers. This latter problem may be made more acute by the fact that initially foreclosed people may appear to possess desirable managerial qualities, such as being decisive and single-minded. Consequently, foreclosed people tend to be strongly represented in positions of power and responsibility.

For the individual to escape from a foreclosed position it is necessary to undergo for a time what is known as *adaptive regression*. It involves regression in the sense of assuming some characteristics of youth, such as seen in the moratorium. It is adaptive because the process can lead to a new and more effective identity. One has to abandon former convictions and admit uncertainty, and many, particularly males, may resist what they see as a sign of weakness. Decisiveness is often perceived as a desirable masculine quality, particularly for those aspiring for senior managerial posts, and research shows that adaptive regression is handled both more easily and more commonly by females (Bilsker and Marcia, 1991).

For society the issue is that men still hold most of the powerful places in politics, business and the professions. Foreclosed males are more likely to be in position to affect others than foreclosed females, as they are the leaders, law-makers and decision takers. Large scale authoritarianism, intolerance and attempts to exercise strong social control over others, as expressed in national politics and legislative frameworks, are most likely to be realized when foreclosed males occupy key positions in that society. It was this possibility that Erikson had in mind in his warning, quoted earlier in this chapter, about those who wage holy wars against others who challenge their beliefs.

Chapter Summary

- There is considerable evidence that adolescents often become engaged with issues of values and beliefs, although they may not be able to articulate an ideological position;
- these beliefs are often very labile;
- Erikson argued that the growth of these beliefs helped the adolescent to respond to the world and to become socialized into their culture;
- Kohlberg developed a model of moral development which has been seriously challenged by Carol Gilligan;
- the implications of Gilligan's work extend to such fields as educational assessment;
- a further conclusion we might reach is about the vulnerability of people who have gained their sense of identity through foreclosure.

Further Reading

BULL, N.J. (1969) *Moral Judgement from Childhood to Adolescence*, London: Routledge Kegan Paul. Obviously, it may be a bit dated, but is good in some aspects, for example, the process of testing for moral development.

FOWLER, J.W., NIPKOW, K.E. and SCHWEITZER, F. (Eds) (1992) *Stages of Faith and Religious Development: Implications for Church, Education and Society*, London: SCM Press. A good contemporary review of the key ideas.

GILLIGAN, C. (1982) *In a Different Voice*, Cambridge, Mass: Harvard University Press. Essential reading.

GIPPS, C. and MURPHY P. (1994) *A Fair Test?*, Buckingham: Open University Press. Extends Gilligan's notion of gendered difference in styles of thinking to responses to educational tests.

KITWOOD, T. (1990) *Concern for Others: A New Psychology of Conscience and Morality*, London: Routledge. The author brings together academic psychology and insights from counselling.

KOHLBERG, L. (1981) *Essays in Moral Development*, San Francisco: Harper Row. Most of Kohlberg's work is scattered through the literature, here there is some attempt to bring it together.

Chapter 8

The Schooling of Adolescents

Schooling, using this word in the broadest sense, has been chosen as the focus of this chapter for it is a universal experience of adolescents and has among its explicit aims the personal development of its students. Many of the significant encounters within this context will be individual as schools are sites in which the peers have the opportunity to meet and relate and in which the young may find the adult role models they seek. But the first theme which I wish to pursue is less on these individual encounters than on schools as social institutions.

The School as a Social Institution

One theme which has emerged in the past two or three decades, both among those critics who despair of conventional schooling and its advocates, has been the potency of the school culture in shaping the young.

On the negative side we have the deschooling movement articulated by such as Ivan Illich and John Holt. Although these two writers end up pursuing similar arguments they started from opposite ends of a spectrum. Illich (1971) worked from an overall concern about the increasing 'institutionalization of values' in which process has become confused with substance. He argued against the notion that the health of a nation can be assessed by its expenditure on medical care, its security by its spending on the military, and the quality of education of its population by the cost of its schools. Affluent societies can spend more on such provision, but the very affluence may cause problems, as with pollution, or allow indulgence, such as with unnecessary cosmetic surgery. His thesis was on the need to return to the basic issues and look at what these bureaucratic providing agencies contribute to the quality of life. His conclusion was that 'for most men the right to learn is curtailed by the obligation to attend school'.

Holt's initial interests were in the specific events occurring in the classroom and asking whether these would motivate learning or not. He looked at these encounters from the student perspective. For example, if someone volunteers an answer to a question and are then rebuked for being wrong, then they may be reluctant to risk another rebuke by participating again, and also be confused in not knowing why their answer was incorrect. He detailed a range of such encounters which might damage the wish to learn. Initially, his motive seemed to be a wish to improve teaching within the conventional school system, but later, notably in Holt (1981), he had despaired of that system and emerged as an advocate of parents assuming the responsibility for education within the home.

The common ground to these two voices is the belief that schools are too large and impersonal and that their organization, with bells ringing every forty minutes to signify the need to move to another task, inhibits learning. They argued that learners themselves are the best judges on how long it is worth pursuing one task and what should follow. As institutions, the argument goes, schools are too marked by competition rather than cooperation, by hierarchies rather than community, by bullying rather than caring. Given these circumstances schools are something to be endured rather than sites facilitating personal and intellectual development.

There may be enough validity in these criticisms for us to attempt to improve practices within our schools, but it is difficult to justify a complete rejection of the conventional system as it provides many positive experiences. These include access to a range of facilities, such as libraries, laboratories and provision for sports. Schools provide opportunities for the social experience of working with peers and allow access to a range of well educated adults who might provide role models of how adult life can be lived. These virtues are so considerable I cannot see any viable alternative to the school in some form. In that case, the key question is what scope is there for making it a better institution.

Probably the best study related to that question comes from Rutter *et al.* (1979). Although the source is somewhat dated, the quality of the research on which it is based makes it particularly valuable. The authors looked at the progress of two thousand secondary school students in twelve inner London schools. Although the schools were in many ways alike, in geographical situation and the social mix of the intake, they varied considerably in their success, whether measured by academic or behavioural criteria. The relative success of a school was not primarily dependent on such obvious variables as the physical conditions or class size, although these affect the ease of the teaching task, but more on its ethos. Three passages from their conclusion are worth quoting:

> . . . schools performed fairly similarly on all the various measures of outcome. That is, schools which did better than average in terms of the children's behaviour in school tended also to do better than average in terms of examination success and delinquency. (p. 178)

> . . . the differences between schools in outcome were systematically related to their characteristics as social institutions. (p. 178)

> The implication is that individual actions or measures may combine to create a particular ethos, or set of values, attitudes and behaviours which will become characteristic of the school as a whole. (p. 179)

Subsequent work in a variety of contexts has tended to confirm these conclusions. For example, within the last decade or two there have been immense differences in the ways we have perceived bullying. Initially, it was attributed to a few children who possessed some personality defect. Then it was recognized that those who were once bullied often became bullies later on, so the description was of a learnt behaviour, passed on from one to another like a contagious disease. More contemporary thinking is revealed in a research report by Cullingford and Morrison (1995), who state that '... bullying was part of the ethos of the schools. The problem is not a matter of isolated incidents and individuals. It is pervasive in the social life of the school, and therefore all children are affected by it in one form or another' (p. 547).

The importance of the overall school ethos has become appreciated in a variety of contexts. As far back as 1975 the Bullock Report, *A Language for Life*, made the point that the mastery of language was far too important an educational goal to be left solely to the provenance of language teachers, and schools needed to adopt policies which involved all the staff. More recently, debates about moral education have taken a similar line, that it was not simply something to be covered in an occasional lesson but needed a consistent school approach, in which practice and precept were congruent.

One of the most formative and depressing experiences in my professional life was doing some work in an institution for young offenders. During the classes and allied activities the teachers lectured the young on the need to become law-abiding citizens and subjected them to a rigid, militaristic discipline, where the boys had to respond to a series of commands. Outside these sessions the boys were ruled by fear and violence imposed by the dominant thugs among their group. On one occasion, two boys were savagely beaten up, and although the incident must have been witnessed by many, no one, not even the victims, would say what happened. The staff could not ascertain who had carried out the violence or why they had done so. Such a regime, where precept and practice are so contradictory, taught the teenagers little, other than that the power of the criminal is more to be feared than that of officials. Government opinion has wavered about the effectiveness of imprisonment. For example, the 1991 Criminal Justice Act steered courts away from handing out custodial sentences, but the 1994 Act reversed this process. Whatever measures, we must surely do better than the institution which I have just described.

The original Rutter study has been misused or misunderstood in two ways. Politicians quote this report and similar research evidence to argue that it does not matter if class sizes increase, as it does not affect performance. If anyone really believed that to be the case then why stop at the incremental increases of about 10 per cent why not double class sizes and halve the bill for teachers' salaries? It is notable that in fee-paying, independent schools, where parents can be said to vote with their cheque books, class sizes tend to be well below the national average.

The second example is that of some tabloid newspapers who seized on a comment made at the time of the report and suggested that all one had to do to create a good school was have a bowl of flowers on display in the foyer. If only it were that easy. The serious point being made was that usually the ethos of the school could be assessed very quickly by its appearance and noise levels. In some instances vandalism and theft caused the school authorities to remove non-essential items, such as the flowers, from public areas.

It is generally agreed that a desirable ethos is established mainly through the efforts of senior staff, who have a clear idea of what they want within the institution, and are able to persuade all staff to be consistent in working within these guidelines.

Certainly, this last point corresponds with what teenagers themselves say. I have found the most commonly quoted attribute of a good teacher is being consistent between pupils, so there are no favourites, and across time so the same rigour applies in lessons from one week to the next. It seems that these adolescents can live, within broad terms, with either strict or more relaxed regimes, but they do need to understand the rules under which they are working. Interestingly, one of the other desirable attributes they mention is teacher competence, as one boy said to me, 'It is my job to muck around. It is the teacher's job to stop me'. Obviously the consistency within the school should be extended as far as possible into the home, so that the adolescent receives similar messages from parents and teachers.

> **Activity**
>
> Try to look at a school you know is if through fresh eyes in order to judge it as a social institution. What do you notice about its appearance, the state of the decor, and the presence of litter? Is it welcoming? What about the noise levels? How do children behave between lessons? What communication do you hear between staff and students? What are the facilities like? You can dig progressively deeper, for example by asking about staff support and training. What are the school policies, for example on bullying, equal opportunities? How do staff talk about students, parents and each other? What do the students say about the school?

Intellectual Take-off

Although teaching adolescents is challenging, it has compensations, one being their sudden growth of interest in ideas and beliefs. After years of sitting in class, doing just enough work to avoid trouble, someone may show a new enthusiasm, wanting to question the teacher about the lesson content, and prepared to argue about meaning and interpretation.

Twenty years ago we would probably have attributed this development to the move from concrete into formal operational thinking. More recently

Figure 6: *Percentage of British children who have reached different Piagetian stages of cognitive development*

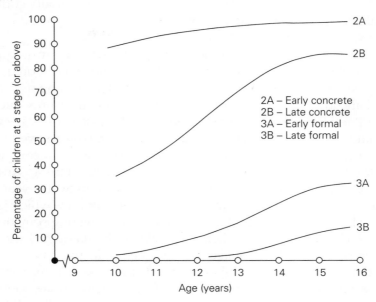

2A – Early concrete
2B – Late concrete
3A – Early formal
3B – Late formal

Source: SHAYER, M. and ADEY, P. (1981) *Towards a Science of Science Teaching*, London: Heinemann.

doubts have surfaced about this notion. Part of the problem is that the description of formal thinking is so sparse, essentially located in Inhelder and Piaget (1958), that it is not clear what constitutes this state within different subject domains. In addition, it was originally assumed that the move into the formal thinking mode is a general characteristic of most adolescents, and some texts of educational psychology still make this assertion despite there being no evidence to support it. The one large-scale study carried out in this country, by Shayer and Adey (1981), suggested that only a minority of adolescents, about 30 per cent at the age of sixteen, reached this stage, as shown in *Figure 6.* Furthermore, the shape of the developmental curves shown in this figure suggested that there was unlikely to be a significant increase in the proportion after the age of sixteen. In this event, we have to think again about adolescent cognitive development.

One possible clue to what is happening comes from their finding that appreciably more boys show formal thinking than girls. This finding is puzzling when we note that girls do much better than boys in the GCSE examinations at the age of sixteen (in 1995 57.1 per cent of the girls gained A to C grades, compared with 48.9 per cent of the boys). One possible explanation is that we have an analogous situation to that of Kohlberg and Gilligan with respect to moral development. Possibly Inhelder and Piaget's description of formal thinking, and hence Shayer and Adey's test instruments, tapped into one strand of more advanced thinking, one more commonly employed by males. The logical demands of formal thinking can be compared with the logical analysis demanded by Kohlberg's taxonomy. In this event, we might postulate that there exists a second mode, corresponding to Gilligan's relational thinking, which is more widely used by girls in academic work.

There is some empirical support for this hypothesis. In a large scale survey of adolescents I identified a small group of girls who scored no more than average for their age on the Shayer and Adey reasoning tests but who were well ahead of the average on certain personality measures, such as the Loevinger Ego Development Test (Loevinger and Wessler, 1970, Loevinger *et al.*, 1970 and 1976). The discrepancy was so large that I interviewed a number of these girls, and they seemed to have two characteristics in common. One was a full understanding of self. The other was to decentre, to understand other people and show empathy. Typical comments from twelve-year-old girls in this group were 'When they avoided me I felt self-pity, which is stupid, but that's what I did', and 'I find myself being overpowering sometimes with Debbie, which I know annoys her, but I still do it, although I try not to'.

The importance of this Piagetian perspective to this book lies in the ongoing debate whether an adolescent needs to possess formal operational thinking as a resource for effective identity development. Enough doubt exists about the adequacy of the concept of formal thinking for us to shift the discussion more to the widening of interests which characterizes many adolescents. Recognition of the possibilities of the wider world may be the more important cognitive resource.

Whatever the explanation, we can recognize the widening of interests, the concern with adult issues, which allows the teaching process to move more towards a discussion among equals, and less of a simple transmission of knowledge. In turn, this brings a change in the social relationship between teacher and student, as roles become redefined.

Failing Pupils

In the first section of this chapter we addressed the notions of success and failure among schools, but within any school there is likely to be a wide diversity in the experience of the pupils. In the 1960s, the decade in which educational sociology mushroomed in this country, the initial explanations for differences in performance were largely in terms of social class. Major figures, such as Halsey and Douglas, drew attention to the spiral of under-achievement which working class pupils were at risk of entering. For example, Douglas (1964) listed the disadvantages such pupils might experience: the absence of books and a quiet place to read at home; the lack of parental interest in academic work or, at least, an inability to help with the work; the difficulties of parents communicating effectively with the teachers in order to cooperate in the education of the young. A series of factors act cumulatively to disadvantage these children.

Subsequently, the concern widened to embrace issues of ethnicity and gender. In the latter case there has been a curious development with most of the concern up to about 1990 being with the apparent academic under-achievement of girls. Since 1990 girls have fared better at the GCSE examinations taken by sixteen-year-old students. In 1995 women became for the first time the majority among university undergraduates and in 1996 the females fared better in the GCE A-level examinations taken by eighteen-year-old students. Some of the causes of this change have already been discussed, notably the loss of job opportunities for young men. The key question is whether this change in the fortune of one sub-group in society can be emulated by others. The failure of social engineering initiatives, such as Head Start in the United States, disillusioned many about the effectiveness of interventions. It seemed as cycles of deprivation were too powerfully entrenched to respond to the limited influence of external intervention. This issue may repay more careful study.

Moving on to the individual student we can recognize some of the requirements for overcoming experience of failure. Learning experiences need to be such that the student can gain some success and acquire a sense of hope. This sense of hope has to be anchored in some reality. If we go back to Mead's (1934) distinction between ideal self and the perception of the real self, then the gap should not be too great. If there is no belief in a better role for the self, if there is no ideal then there is no goal, and no motivation. Some gap between the perceptions of the ideal and real self is necessary as stimulus to effort. If, however, the gap appears too large, so that any worth-while goal seems to be beyond the competence of the student, then again motivation is lost. The task of teachers is to encourage students to set them-selves goals which are challenging but realizable.

Some pupils fare poorly within the school system. Long term exclusions from school now run at between eleven and thirteen thousand each year, and once the young people have been excluded all the attention they are likely to receive will be two hours tutorial assistance each day. For the rest of the time they may well be on the streets unless parents intervene, yet too often poor parental control was a major causal factor in their situation.

With all students cooperation between schools and parents is crucial, hence the recent rise in the notion of 'positive parenting', in which the role and duties of parenthood are emphasized. Increasingly, schools are asking parents to enter into a contract in which parents agree to undertake certain duties, for example, ensuring pupils attend school regularly, wear appropriate clothing and carry out homework.

The effects of the absence of the parent are revealed most vividly in the abject failure of students in children's homes to achieve average grades in school work. My criticism is not of the residential social workers, who are poorly paid and often overworked, but more of a system in which young people are likely to be frequently moved from home to home. Even with a home they cannot easily develop a close relationship with an adult as staff work on a shift system so that different carers assume responsibility at different times throughout the day.

Promoting Self Development

Two of the general requirements for a school to provide an effective forum for adolescent development have already been discussed in this chapter. The first task is the establishment of a helpful ethos, in which personal freedom is balanced against a framework of recognized rules and procedures, and where effective communication exists, among teachers and between teachers and students. The second need is an evolution in the rules and in the relationships between staff and the young, so that the growing maturity of the adolescents is recognized. Those familiar with the Rosenthal and Jacobson (1968) work *Pygmalion in the Classroom* will have encountered the notion that adolescents will tend to conform to our expectations of them. If treated as immature and irresponsible then they are more likely to remain so.

Increasingly, as they mature, we should help the students feel that they 'own' their newly acquired knowledge. By this term we mean that they should not see lesson content being presented on a take-it or leave-it basis, something to be assimilated simply because the teacher says so, but as something relevant, useful and valuable to them. They need to integrate this new material with their prior knowledge so that the new becomes fully meaningful to them. This process of recognizing that some of what is being learnt as being relevant and useful, while perceiving other as less valuable, helps develop awareness of themselves and what they value. Owned knowledge is likely to be valued, and knowing what one values is part of a personal identity. In addition, with maturation students can develop habits of metacognition, the thinking about thinking, so that they monitor their own learning, and can recognize whether they are learning effectively or not.

Schools should seek to inform students about the world. How can one make a career choice without knowing what the possibilities are, and what each of these require, for example in terms of academic qualifications? This need can be met in a variety of ways, with a well stocked resource centre, work experience, personal guidance, and possibly the use of psychological tests of aptitudes and interests. Vocational guidance is readily easy to define and provide. It is not so obvious how other aspects of personal identity development can be helped.

Dreyer (1994) lists the qualities of an identity-enhancing school curriculum. These are:

1   It is a curriculum which 'promotes exploration, responsible choice and self-determination by students'. He goes on to suggest 'the young person must be able to understand the alternatives, evaluate each one systematically, and feel a sense of personal control over the decisions he or she makes' (p. 129).

2 The curriculum 'promotes role playing and social interaction across generations' (p. 131). Entering adulthood involves assuming new roles and some active exploration of the possibilities is necessary.

3 Such a curriculum 'promotes the student's understanding of time and how the past is related to the present' (p. 132). Here he is concerned with the match between one's personal time, the opportunities of a lifetime, and the circumstances of our contemporary society. A mismatch means that the individual feels alienated from the present and can see no satisfactory role for oneself.

4 'An identity-enhancing curriculum promotes self-acceptance and positive feedback from teachers and counselors' (p. 136). This need was argued in the last section of this chapter.

Teachers with pastoral responsibilities, and particularly the Personal and Social Education (PSE) teachers, should take a lead in addressing these issues, but, as argued before with respect to language education, the task is too great to be covered by a few staff within a few lessons. Again it is a whole school matter. With the pressure for schools to demonstrate their success in the league tables of GCSE and A-level passes, those parts of the curriculum which do not directly contribute to this effort tend to be given a lower priority. Schools vary in the time for PSE provision, the content, staff training and staff support. Increasingly, students aged over sixteen are entering Further Education colleges rather than staying on in their secondary school. In many respects the college ambience may be more suitable for these adolescents, but one possible drawback is that the PSE function is pushed further into the background.

Handling sensitive issues, such as family responsibilities, personal beliefs, and sexuality requires special techniques. If simply asked to talk about such matters a group of adolescents are likely to fall into embarrassed silence. Partly, they are silent because they do not want to reveal things about themselves and their families. But, additionally, they may be uncertain how to handle this particular discourse. Within conventional lessons the roles of the teachers and students are clear, and the lesson task is clear, but PSE sessions may appear confusing. The teacher may seem reluctant to take a lead and carry out the expected didactic role. Students may be asked to talk about issues, which they have not yet thought fully about, and for which they do not possess the appropriate language. Often the adolescents, who sat silent in a lesson, will say afterwards that they now know what they want to contribute to the discussion, having had time to think matters through and find the words to articulate their ideas.

There are a number of techniques which can be used to help people enter such discussions. Some, such as the use of T groups, I would argue are inappropriate for use in a school, as they may cause a student to reveal more about the self than he or she can handle in subsequent meetings with peers and the teacher. Role plays work well, provided a few key guidelines are set up. There must be ground rules for the discussion, to avoid descent into verbal abuse. The students playing the roles should be given some briefing, so that they can build their arguments on a factual base. It is best to provide the notes in advance so that they have time to consider how they will argue their case. Most crucially of all, roles should be cast against type. If an adolescent is concerned about a sensitive issue in their life, for example, uncertainty about their sexual orientation, and are then asked to play a role of someone facing the same issue, then role and reality become confused. The student maybe forced to articulate certain sentiments before they are ready to do so, and have to deal with the hostile reactions of others within the role play. If people are cast against their real type then they can separate criticism of the role they played from criticism of themselves in real life. The distinction can be reinforced by asking students to wear a label with their assumed name while acting in the play. In this situation criticisms should be addressed to the name on the label, not to the actor.

If these procedures seem too elaborate then even the provision of simple stimulus material, such as a newspaper article on a current controversial issue, may be enough to provoke a good discussion. The article might provide some factual evidence to inform the discussion and also act as a distancing device, so the discussion is centred on people and events outside the school.

For those having a one-to-one counselling role there are two golden rules. Confidentiality should be respected, although there are legal difficulties if you are informed about child abuse and fail to act on the information. Secondly, there is no point in criticizing or moralizing. The adolescent probably already knows that he or she has behaved foolishly, that is precisely why they have sought advice, so reinforcing their negative feelings about themselves does nothing to help them. What they need is the opportunity to talk through the problem with someone who listens sympathetically and practical advice about how they can next proceed.

Support Agencies

Working in a counselling or pastoral role raises a range of possible problems such that one may need to admit the limits of coping. Part of our function is to act as a conduit and pass the troubled adolescent on to someone else for specialist help. Obviously, this move can only be undertaken with the knowledge and approval of the adolescent involved. Sometimes a medical practitioner may be needed to deal with such matters as anorexia, drug abuse, pregnancy or concern about venereal disease and HIV/AIDS. Sometimes the youngster would benefit from meeting peers in a similar situation and gain from support of such a group. Sometimes we encounter situations which are so far removed from our own experience that we feel incompetent to offer help.

Institutions, such as a school, should have established procedures for involving support agencies. A senior member of staff should have a list of support agencies and be able to advise on their use. Other starting points include the local Citizen's Advice Bureau and the Social Services Department of the local government. The public library should carry a list of agencies in the area. In the past, Local Education Authorities provided a range of support, including the use of educational psychologists, but in recent years the changes

---

Activity

In any event, it is sensible to compile a list of local resources for your own use if you are involved in pastoral work. In order to facilitate the process I have provided a list of possible agencies, which is not meant to be comprehensive but illustrative. I have not given telephone numbers and addresses, partly because these often change, partly because you need local information.

Alcoholics Anonymous—not just for adolescents themselves, often for a parent.

Anorexics Aid—self-help groups and support.

Brook Advisory Centres—advice on contraception, abortion and pregnancy.

Childline—intended for direct use by children and young people.

Citizens Advice Centre

Family Planning Association

Family Welfare Association

Friend—support for gay and lesbian people.

Gingerbread—support and information for single mothers.

Grapevine—teenage pregnancy, offers peer counselling for adolescents.

Incest Crisis Line

Lesbian and Gay Switchboard—the London office has information on local support groups.

Narcotics Anonymous

NSPCC—produces materials for teachers.

Neighbourhood Law Centre

Nightline—many institutions within higher education offer peer telephone counselling and support groups.

Rape Crisis Centre

Relate—formerly the Marriage Guidance Council, now helps with a range of relationship problems.

Release—particularly concerned with drugs, police powers etc.

Samaritans—although focused on possible suicide cases they do help those with less urgent problems.

Terence Higgins Trust—information and help relating to HIV/AIDS.

In addition to these organizations, one may make use of local religious groups, and local hospitals. The local government should provide youth services, but the extent of provision is variable.

in funding of these authorities and schools may have led to a loss of some of these services. In any event, the crucial message is that you are not on your own. There are sources of assistance.

Chapter Summary

- School effectiveness should not be judged solely by tables of academic achievement but also assess the effectiveness in helping individual student development;
- schools are important in being part of the universal experience of adolescents and in providing an 'institutionalized moratorium';
- schools are powerful agents of socialization in which the dominant school ethos is crucial;
- positive steps can be taken, within the curriculum and in pupil–staff interactions to help adolescent identity development;
- PSE teachers and those undertaking pastoral functions should have access to a network of help agencies.

Further Reading

ARCHER, S.L. (Ed) (1994) *Interventions for Adolescent Identity Development*, Newbury Park, CA: Sage. An essential text.

BURNS, R. (1982) *Self-Concept Development and Education*, London: Holt, Rinehart and Winston. Slightly dated, but wide-ranging survey, with attention paid to school and classroom practices.

GALLOWAY, D. (1990) *Pupil Welfare and Counselling: An Approach to Personal and Social Education Across the Curriculum*, Harlow: Longmans. Sets the British educational context well.

MONCK, E. (Ed) (1988) *Emotional and Behavioural Problems* in *Adolescence: Course Leaders Pack/Guide*, Windsor: Nelson-NFER. Contains material on dealing with topics such as substance abuse, sexuality, sexual abuse, living with marital breakdown, disruptive behaviour and eating disorders.

SHAPP, S. and SMITH, P. (1994) *Tackling Bullying in Your School: A Practical Handbook*, London: Routledge. Bullying is not only an important issue in itself but effectively illuminates the dynamics of schools.

Chapter 9

Conclusion: Adolescence Today

In the first chapter of this book the current concern about adolescent behaviour was reviewed and set into a historical context. The question was raised whether the problems young people face nowadays are more challenging than before. It should have become evident from the subsequent chapters that there are no easy answers to such a question.

If we look at just one factor, that of material wealth, then the average teenager is now better off than those in the past. However, we have had in the last fifteen years an increasing diversity in income. More people will be relatively worse off, using that term to describe those who earn less than half the national average. Furthermore, more teenagers are probably worse off in absolute terms, as changes in the social welfare system has reduced entitlement for those aged between sixteen and eighteen. The increased number of young people sleeping rough and begging in our cities testify to this effect. Therefore we have a situation in which many adolescents are able to wear designer clothes and can afford to go to discos and raves, and spend money on drugs, while others may well suffer from under nourishment.

If we pursue this issue of poverty in more detail then more complexities emerge. About four-fifths of people within the poorest 20 per cent of the families in this country are law-abiding. The remaining 20 per cent of the people in this poorest 20 per cent make up well over half the long-term criminally active population. In other words, poverty is a risk factor in criminality, but there is no simple, direct effect. The majority of the poor remain honest. Evidence such as this illustrates the difficulty in generalizing.

Remembering the diversity of the adolescent experience, according to such variables as ethnicity, class and gender, we might conclude that we cannot generalize. It might be argued that all that we can do is report on case studies of specific sub-groups in our society. While recognizing the strength of this argument, and the need to recognize this diversity, it can still be maintained that in many respects adolescence is a universal experience. The effects of puberty, the ending of schooling and the need to enter the labour market are three of these universal variables. The notion of identity achievement is applicable to all.

Another universal factor for contemporary adolescents is that they are entering a social world which is itself in flux. Insecurity within the labour market and marriage makes it increasingly likely that adolescents cannot plan with any certainty for their entire adult life, but have to make identity decisions which might work out for them for a period of five or ten years. This consideration means that in turn adults will have to be prepared to redefine themselves at intervals. In this event, the task for the adolescent may be measured less in what is chosen, but more in the quality of the choice process. Those who foreclose on their identity will be at risk as circumstances may later force change on them. Increasingly, young people will have to enter adulthood with the necessary flexibility to deal positively with social change. This need probably represents the main difference between adolescence today and the experience we adults had in our youth. Compared with previous generations the young probably have more opportunities but enjoy less certainties. To what extent contemporary adolescents are to be envied or gain our sympathy is an issue I will leave the reader to ponder.

Bibliography

ADAMS, G.R. (1985) 'Identity and political socialization', in WATERMAN, A.S. (Ed) *Identity in Adolescence: Processes and Content*, San Francisco: Jossey-Bass.

ADAMS, G.R. (1992) 'Introduction and Overview', in ADAMS, G.R., GULLOTTA, T.P. and MONTEMAYOR, R. (Eds) *Adolescent Identity Formation*, Newbury Park, CA: Sage.

ADAMS, G.R., GULLOTTA, T.P. and MONTEMAYOR, R. (Eds) (1992) *Adolescent Identity Formation*, Newbury Park, CA: Sage.

AGGLETON, P. (1987) *Rebels Without a Cause? Middle Class Youth, and the Transition from School to Work*, Lewes: Falmer Press.

ARCHER, S.L. (Ed) (1994) *Interventions for Adolescent Identity Development*, Thousand Oaks, CA: Sage.

ASKEW, S. and ROSS, C. (1988) *Boys Don't Cry: Boys and Sexism in Education*, Milton Keynes: Open University Press.

AUDEN, W.H. (1936) 'Letter to Lord Byron', as reprinted in MENDESON, E. (Ed) *The English Auden*, London: Faber, 1977.

AVERY, A.W. (1982) 'Escaping loneliness in adolescence: The case for androgyny', *Journal of Youth and Adolescence*, **11**, pp. 451–9.

BANKS, M., BATES, I., BREAKWELL, G., BYNNER, J., EMLER, N., JAMIESON, L. and ROBERTS, K. (1992) *Careers and Identities*, Milton Keynes: Open University Press.

BARNETT, C. (1986) *The Audit of War: The Illusion and Reality of Britain as a Great Nation*, London: Macmillan.

BEAUVOIR, S. DE (1949) *The Second Sex*, London: Cape.

BELL, N.J. and BELL, R.W. (Eds) (1993) *Adolescent Risk Taking*, Newbury Park, CA: Sage.

BEM, S.L. (1974) 'The measurement of clinical androgyny', *Journal of Consulting and Clinical Psychology*, **42**, pp. 155–62.

BEM, S.L. (1975) 'Sex-role adaptability: One consequence of psychological androgyny', *Journal of Personal and Social Psychology*, **31**, pp. 634–43.

BERNARD, H.S. (1981) 'Identity formation during late adolescence; A review of some empirical findings', *Adolescence*, **16**, pp. 349–58.

BILKSER, D. and MARCIA, J.E. (1991) 'Adaptive regression and ego identity', *Journal of Adolescence*, **14**, pp. 75–84.

BLOS, P. (1962) *On Adolescence: A Psychoanalytic Interpreation*, New York: Collier-Macmillan.

BOURNE, E. (1978) 'The state of research on ego identity; A review and appraisal', *Journal of Youth and Adolescence*, Part 1, 7, pp. 223–52, Part 2, 7, pp. 371–92.

BREAKWELL, G. (1986) *Coping with Threatened Identities*, London: Methuen.

BROVERMAN, I.K., BROVERMAN, D.M., CLARKSON, F.E., ROSENKRANTZ, P.S. and VOGEL, S.R. (1970) 'Sex role stereotypes and clinical judgments of mental health', *Journal of Consulting and Clinical Psychology*, **34**, pp. 1–7.

BULL, N.J. (1969) *Moral Judgement from Childhood to Adolescence*, London: Routledge Kegan Paul.

BURNS, R. (1982) *Self-Concept Development and Education*, London: Holt, Rinehart and Winston.

CAMPBELL, E., ADAMS, G.R. and DOBSON, W.R. (1984) 'Family correlates of identity formation in late adolescence: A study of the predictive utility of connectedness and individuality in family relations', *Journal of Youth and Adolescence*, **13**, pp. 509–25.

CAPLAN, P.J. (1979) 'Erikson's concept of inner space: A data-based reevaluation', *American Journal of Orthopsychiatry*, **49**, pp. 100–8.

CENTRAL STATISTICAL OFFICE (1995) *Social Trends 25*, London: HMSO.

CENTRAL STATISTICAL OFFICE (1996) *Social Trends 26*, London: HMSO.

CHARLESWORH, W.R. and LA FRENIER, P. (1983) 'Dominance, friendship utilization and resource utilization in preschool children's groups', *Ethology and Sociobiology*, **4**, pp. 175–86.

CHODOROW, N. (1978) *The Reproduction of Mothering: Psychoanalysis and the Sociology of Gender*, Berkeley: University of California Press.

COFFIELD, F., BORRILL, C. and MARSHALL, S. (1986) *Growing Up at the Margins*, Milton Keynes: Open University Press.

COLEMAN, J.C. (1974) *Relationships in Adolescence*, London: Routledge Kegan Paul.

COLEMAN, J.C. and HENDRY, L. (1990) *The Nature of Adolescence*, London: Routledge.

COTE, J.E. and LEVINE, C. (1983) 'Marcia and Erikson: The relationship among ego identity statuses, neuroticism, dogmatism and purpose in life', *Journal of Youth and Adolescence*, **12**, pp. 43–53.

COTTERELL, J. (1996) *Social Networks and Social Influences in Adolescence*, London: Routledge.

COYLE, A. (1988) 'An investigation of the ordering of key events in gay identity formation', Talk given at the London meeting of the British Psychological Society.

CRAIG-BRAY, L., ADAMS, G.R. and DOBSON, W.R. (1988) 'Identity formation and social relations during late adolescence', *Journal of Youth and Adolescence*, **17**, pp. 173–87.

CULLINGFORD, C. and MORRISON, J. (1995) 'Bullying as a formative influence: The relationship between the experience of school and criminality', *British Educational Research Journal*, **21**, pp. 547–60.

DAVIS, J. (1990) *Youth and the Condition of Britain: Images of Adolescent Conflict*, London: Athlone Press.

DEWEY, J. (1916) *Democracy and Education*, New York: The Free Press.

DILLARD, A. (1987) *An American Childhood*, New York: Harper and Row.

DOUGLAS, J.W.B. (1964) *The Home and the School: A Study of Ability and Attainment*, London: MacGibbon and Kee.

DOUVAN, E. and ADELSON, J. (1966) *The Adolescent Experience*, New York: Wiley.

DOWRICK, S. (1992) *Intimacy and Solitude*, London: The Women's Press.

DREYER, P.H. (1994) 'Designing curricular identity interventions' in ARCHER S.L. (Ed) *Interventions for Adolescent Identity Development*, Thousand Oaks, CA: Sage.

EIDUSON, B.T. (1962) *Scientists: Their Psychological World*, New York: Basic Books.

ELKIND, D. (1970) *Children and Adolescents*, New York: Oxford University Press.

EOC/OFSTED (1996) *The Gender Divide: Performance Differences Between Boys and Girls at School*, London: HMSO.

ERIKSON, E.H. (1950) *Childhood and Society*, New York: Norton.

ERIKSON, E.H. (1964) *Insight and Responsibility*, New York: Norton.

ERIKSON, E.H. (1968) *Identity, Youth and Crisis*, New York: Norton.

ERIKSON, E.H. (1974) *Dimensions of a New Identity*, New York: Norton.

ERIKSON, E.H. (1985) *The Life Cycle Completed*, New York: Norton.

FINKELHOR, D. (1990) 'Early and long-term effects of child sexual abuse: An update', *Professional Psychology: Research and Practice*, **21**, pp. 325–30.

FOUCAULT, M. (1977–79) *The History of Sexuality*, Volumes 1 to 3, Harmondsworth: Penguin.

FOWLER, J.W., NIPKOW, K.E. and SCHWEITZER, F. (Eds) (1992) *Stages of Faith and Religious Development: Implications for Church, Education and Society*, London: SCM Press.

FREIRE, P. (1996) *Pedagogy of the Oppressed*, revised edition, London: Penguin Books.

FREUD, A. (1937) *The Ego and the Mechanisms of Defence*, London: Hogarth Press. (Initially published in German in 1936).

FREUD, S. (1923) 'The Ego and the Id', in *On Metapsychology*, Standard Edition, Harmondsworth: Penguin. (Originally published in German in 1923.)

FREUD, S. (1977) *Three Essays on the Theory of Sexuality*, Standard Edition, London: Hogarth Press.

FRIEDENBERG, E.Z. (1959) *The Vanishing Adolescent*, Boston: Beacon Press.

FRYER, D. and ULLAH, P. (1987) *Unemployed People: Social and Psychological Perspectives*, Milton Keynes: Open University Press.

GADDIS, A. and BROOKS-GUNN, J. (1985) 'The male experience of pubertal change', *Journal of Youth and Adolescence*, **14**, pp. 61–9.

GALINSKY, M.D. and FAST, I. (1966) 'Vocational choices as a focus of the identity search', *Journal of Counselling Psychology*, **13**, pp. 89–92.

GALLOWAY, D. (1990) *Pupil Welfare and Counselling: An Approach to Personal and Social Education Across the Curriculum*, Harlow: Longmans.

GAOTTI, K.M., KOZBERG, S.F. and FARMER, M.C. (1991) 'Gender and developmental differences in adolescent's conceptions of moral reasoning', *Journal of Youth and Adolescence*, **20**, pp. 13–30.

GARDNER, P.L. (1975) 'Attitudes to science: A review', *Studies in Science Education*, **2**, pp. 1–41.

GILLIGAN, C. (1982a) *In a Different Voice*, Cambridge, MS: Harvard University Press.

GILLIGAN, C. (1982b) 'Why should a woman be more like a man?', *Psychology Today*, **16**, pp. 68–77.

GILLIGAN, C. and ATTANUCCI, J. (1988) 'Two moral orientations: Gender differences and similarities', *Merrill-Palmer Quarterly*, **34**, pp. 223–37.

GIPPS, C. and MURPHY, P. (1994) *A Fair Test? Assessment, Achievement and Equity*, Buckingham: Open University Press.

GREENWOOD, J.D. (1994) *Realism, Identity and Emotion: Reclaiming Social Psychology*, London: Sage.

HALL, G.S. (1904) *Adolescence: Its Psychology and its Relations with Physiology, Anthropology, Sex, Crime, Religion and Education*, New York: Appleton.

HARDING, J. (Ed) (1986) *Perspectives on Gender and Science*, Lewes: Falmer Press.

HAYES, R.L. (1982) 'A review of adolescent identity formation: Implications for education', *Adolescence*, **17**, pp. 153–65.

HEAD, J. (1979) 'Personality and the pursuit of science', *Studies in Science Education*, **6**, pp. 23–44.

HEAD, J. (1980) 'A model to link personality characteristics to a preference for science', *European Journal of Science Education*, **2**, pp. 295–300.

HEAD, J. (1985) *The Personal Response to Science*, Cambridge: Cambridge University Press.

HEAD, J. and RAMSDEN, J. (1990) 'Gender, psychological type and science', *International Journal of Science Education*, **12**, pp. 115–21.

HEAD, J., HILL, F. and MAGUIRE, M. (1996) 'Stress and the post graduate secondary school trainee teacher: A British case study', *Journal of Education for Teaching*, **22**, pp. 71–84.

HENDRY, L.B., SHUCKSMITH, J., LOVE, J.G. and GLENDINNING, A. (1993) *Young People's Leisure and Lifestyles*, London: Routledge.

HILL, F. (1995) 'The provision of HIV/AIDS education in English colleges of further education', *Research in Science Education*, **25**, pp. 231–8.

HODGSON, J.W. and FISCHER, J.L. (1979) 'Sex differences in identity and intimacy development', *Journal of Youth and Adolescence*, **8**, pp. 37–50.

HOGG M.A. and ABRAMS, D. (1988) *Social Identifications*, London: Routledge.

HOLLAND, J., RAMAZANOGLU, C. and SHARPE, S. (1993) *Wimp or Gladiator: Contradictions in Acquiring Masculine Identity*, London: Tufnell Press.

HOLLAND, R. (1977) *Self and Social Context*, London: Macmillan.

HOLT, J. (1964) *How Children Fail*, New York: Pitman.

HOLT, J. (1981) *Teach Your Own: A Hopeful Path for Education*, Brightlinsea: Lighthouse Books.

HOOD, J.C. (1993) *Men, Work and Family*, Newbury Park, CA: Sage.

HORNER, M.S. (1972) 'Towards an understanding of achievement-related conflicts in women', *Journal of Social Issues*, **28**, pp. 157–75.

HUDSON, L. (1968) *Frames of Mind*, London: Methuen.

HUTT, C. (1979) 'Sex role differentiation in social development', in McGURK, H. (Ed) *Issues in Childhood Social Development*, London: Methuen.

ILLICH, I.D. (1971) *Deschooling Society*, London: Calder and Boyars.

INHELDER, B. and PIAGET, J. (1958) *The Growth of Logical Thinking*, London: Routledge Kegan Paul.

JACOBY, R. (1975) *Social Amnesia: A Critique of Conformist Psychology from Adler to Laing*, Boston: Beacon Press.

JAQUES, E. (1965) 'Death and the mid-life crisis', *International Journal of Psycho-analysis*, **46**, pp. 502–14.

JOSSELSON, R., GREENBERGER, E. and McCONOCHIE, D. (1977) 'Phenomenological aspects of psychosocial maturity in adolescence', 1 Boys, *Journal of Youth and Adolescence*, **6**, pp. 25–56, and 2 Girls, *Journal of Youth and Adolescence*, **6**, pp. 145–68.

KACERGUIS, M.A. and DAMS, G.R. (1980) 'Erikson stage resolution: The relationship between identity and intimacy', *Journal of Youth and Adolescence*, **2**, pp. 117–25.

KAMPTNER, N.L. (1988) 'Identity development in late adolescence: Causal modelling of social and familial influences', *Journal of Youth and Adolescence*, **17**, pp. 493–514.

KEGAN, R. (1982) *The Evolving Self*, Cambridge, MS: Harvard University Press.

KELLY, A. (Ed) (1987) *Science for Girls?*, Milton Keynes: Open University Press.

KIELL, N. (1967) *The Adolescent Through Fiction: A Psychological Approach*, New York: International Universities Press.

KIELL, N. (1969) *The Universal Experience of Adolescence*, London: University of London Press.

KITWOOD, T. (1990) *Concern for Others: A New Psychology of Conscience and Morality*, London: Routledge.

KITZINGER, C. (1987) *The Social Construction of Lesbianism*, London: Sage.

KLEIN, M. (1932) *The Psychoanalysis of Children*, London: Hogarth Press.

KOHLBERG, L. (1981) *Essays in Moral Development*, San Francisco: Harper Row.

KROGER, J. (1996) *Identity in Adolescence: The Balance Between Self and Other*, 2nd ed., London: Routledge.

KUBIE, L.S. (1954) 'Some unsolved problems of a scientific career', *American Scientist*, **42**, pp. 104–12.

KUHN, D., NASH, C.S. and BRUCKEN, L. (1978) 'Sex role concepts of two- and three-year olds', *Child Development*, **49**, pp. 495–97.

LAMKE, L.K. (1992) 'Adjustment and sex role orientation in adolescence', *Journal of Youth and Adolescence*, **11**, pp. 247–59.

LA VOIE, J.C. (1976) 'Ego identity formation in middle adolescence', *Journal of Youth and Adolescence*, **5**, pp. 371–85.

LEES, S. (1986) *Losing Out*, London: Hutchinson.

LEVER, J. (1976) 'Sex differences in the games children play', *Social Problems*, **23**, pp. 478–87.

LOEVINGER, J. and WESSLER, R. (1970) *Measuring Ego Development I*, San Francisco: Jossey-Bass.

LOEVINGER, J., WESSLER, R. and REDMORE, C. (1970) *Measuring Ego Development II*, San Francisco: Jossey-Bass.

LOEVINGER, J. (1976) *Ego Development: Conceptions and Theories*, San Francisco: Jossey-Bass.

LOGAN, R.D. (1983) 'A re-conceptualization of Erikson's identity stage', *Adolescence*, **18**, pp. 943–6.

LYNN, D.B. (1962) 'Sex-role and parental identification', *Child Development*, **33**, pp. 555–64.

MACCOBY, E.E. and JACKLIN, C.N. (1975) *The Psychology of Sex Differences*, Oxford: Oxford University Press.

MACCOBY, E.E. and JACKLIN, C.N. (1987) 'Gender segregation in childhood', in REESE, E.H. (Ed) *Advances in Child Development and Behavior* (Volume 20), New York: Academic Press.

MALZ, D. and BORKER, R. (1983) 'A cultural approach to male–female miscommunication', in GUMPERZ, J. (Ed) *Language and Social Identity*, Cambridge: Cambridge University Press.

MANCASTER, G. (1977) *Adolescent Development and the Life Tasks*, Boston: Allyn and Bacon.

MARCIA, J.E. (1966) 'Development and validation of ego-identity statuses', *Journal of Personality and Social Psychology*, **3**, pp. 551–8.

MARCIA, J.E. (1976) 'Identity six years after: A follow-up study', *Journal of Youth and Adolescence*, **5**, pp. 145–59.

MARCIA, J.E. (1980) 'Identity in adolescence', in ADELSON, J. (Ed) *Handbook of Adolescent Psychology*, New York: Wiley.

MASLOW, A.H. (1966) *The Psychology of Science: A Reconnaissance*, New York: Harper Row.

Masson, J.M. (1984) *The Assault on Truth: Freud's Suppression of the Seduction Theory*, London: Faber.

Matteson, D.P. (1975) *Adolescence Today: Sex Roles and the Search for Identity*, Homewood, Ill: Dorsey Press.

Mead, G.H. (1934) *Mind, Self and Society*, Chicago: University of Chicago Press.

Mellor, S. (1989) 'Gender differences in identity formation as a function of self-other relationships', *Journal of Youth and Adolescence*, **18**, pp. 361–75.

Miller, D. (1969) *The Age Between: Adolescents in a Disturbed Society*, London: Hutchinson.

Miller, P. McC. and Plant, T. (1996) 'Drinking, smoking and illicit drug use among 15- and 16-year-olds in the United Kingdom', *British Medical Journal*, **313**, pp. 394–7.

Mitchell, J. (1975) *Psychoanalysis and Feminism*, Harmondsworth: Penguin.

Monck, E. (Ed) (1988) *Emotional and Behavioural Problems in Adolescence: Course Leader Guide/Pack*, Windsor: Nelson-NFER.

Montemayor, R. (1994) 'The study of personal relationships during adolescence', in Montemayor, R., Adams, G.R. and Gullotta, T.P. (Eds) *Personal Relationships During Adolescence*, Thousand Oaks, CA: Sage.

Montemayor, R., Adams, G.R. and Gullotta, T.P. (Eds) (1994) *Personal Relationships During Adolescence*, Thousand Oaks, CA: Sage.

Moore, S. and Rosenthal, D. (1993) *Sexuality in Adolescence*, London: Routledge.

Murphy, P.F. and Gipps, C.V. (1996) *Equity in the Classroom: Towards and Effective Pedagogy for Boys and Girls*, London: Falmer Press.

Murray, C. and Dawson, A. (1983) *Five Thousand Adolescents: Their Attitudes, Characteristics and Attainments*, Manchester: Manchester University Press.

Musgrove, F. (1964) *Youth and Social Order*, London: Routledge Kegan Paul.

Nayak, A. and Kehily, M.J. (1996) 'Playing it straight: Masculinities, homophobia and schooling', *Journal of Gender Studies*, **5**, pp. 211–30.

Orlofsky, J.L., Marcia, J.E. and Lesser, I.M. (1973) 'Ego identity status and intimacy versus isolation crisis in young adulthood', *Journal of Personality and Social Psychology*, **27**, pp. 211–9.

Osipow, S.H. (1975) 'The relevance of theories of career development to special groups: Problems, needed data and implications', in Picou, S. and Campbell, R. (Eds) *Career Behavior of Special Groups*, Columbus, Ohio: Merrill.

Parker, M.S. (1985) 'Identity and the development of religious thinking', in Waterman, A.S. (Ed) *Identity in Adolescence, Processes and Contents, Child Development Vol 30*, San Francisco: Jossey-Bass.

Piaget, J. (1932) *The Moral Judgement of the Child*, London: Routledge Kegan Paul.

Prendergast, S. (1992) *'This Is the Time to Grow Up: Girl's Experience of Menstruation in School*, Cambridge: Centre for Family Research.

Raskin, P.M. (1985) 'Identity and vocational development', in Waterman, A.S. (Ed) *Identity in Adolescence, Processes and Contents*, San Francisco: Jossey-Bass.

Raskin, P.M. (1989) 'Identity status research: Implications for career counselling', *Journal of Adolescence*, **12**, pp. 375–88.

Rekers, G.A. and Yates, C.E. (1976) 'Sex-typed play in feminoid boys versus normal boys and girls', *Journal of Abnormal Child Psychology*, **4**, pp. 1–8.

Roberts, K. and Parsell, G. (1988) *Opportunity Structures and Career Trajectories for Age 16–19* (ESRC 16–19 Initiative Occasional Paper), London: City University.

ROBERTS, K., PARSELL, G. and CONNOLLY, O. (1989) *British Economic Recovery: The New Demographic Trend and Young People's Transition into the Labour Market*, (ESRC 16–19 Intitiative Occasional Paper) London: City University.

ROGOW, A.M., MARCIA, J.E. and SLUGOSKI, B.R. (1983) 'The relative importance of identity status interview components', *Journal of Youth and Adolescence*, **12**, pp. 387–400.

ROSENTHAL, D.A., GURNEY, R.A. and MOORE, S.M. (1981) 'From trust to intimacy: A new inventory for examining Erikson's stages of psychosocial development', *Journal of Youth and Adolescence*, **10**, pp. 525–37.

ROSENTHAL, R. and JACOBSON, L. (1966) 'Teacher's expectancies: Determinants of pupils' I.Q. gains', *Psychological Reports*, **19**, pp. 115–8.

ROWE, I. and MARCIA, J.E. (1980) 'Ego identity status, formal operations and moral development', *Journal of Youth and Adolescence*, **9**, pp. 87–99.

RUTTER, M., MAUGHAN, B., MORTIMORE, P. and OUSTON, J. (1979) *Fifteen Thousand Hours: Secondary Schools and Their Effects on Children*, Shepton Mallet: Open Books.

SALISBURY, J. and JACKSON, D. (1996) *Challenging Macho Values: Practical Ways of Working with Adolescent Boys*, London: Falmer Press.

SAMPSON, E.E. (1989) 'The deconstruction of self', in SHOTTER, J. and GERGEN, K.J. (Eds) *Texts of Identity*, London: Sage.

SCHIBECI, R.A. (1984) 'Attitudes to science: An update', *Studies in Science Education*, **11**, pp. 26–59.

SCHOFIELD, M. (1965) *The Sexual Behaviour of Young People*, London: Longmans.

SELKOW, P. (1984) *Assessing Sex Bias in Testing*, Westport: Greenwood Press.

SHAPP, S. and SMITH, P. (1994) *Tackling Bullying in Your School: A Practical Handbook*, London: Routledge.

SHAYER, M. and ADEY, P. (1981) *Towards a Science of Science Teaching: Cognitive Development and Curriculum Demand*, London: Heinemann.

SMITH, C. and LLOYD, B.B. (1978) 'Maternal behaviour and perceived sex of infant', *Child Development*, **49**, pp. 1263–5.

SPACKS, P.M. (1982) *The Adolescent Idea*, London: Faber.

STANWORTH, M. (1983) *Gender and Schooling: A Study of Sexual Division in the Classroom*, London: Hutchinson.

STEVENS, R. (Ed) (1996) *Understanding the Self*, London: Sage (in association with The Open University).

STORR, A. (1988) *Solitude*, New York: Free Press.

SUPER, P.E. (1957) *The Psychology of Careers*, New York: Harper Row.

TAJFEL, H. (Ed) (1978) *Differentiation Between Social Groups: Studies in the Social Psychology of Intergroup Relations*, London: Academic Press.

TRENCHARD, L. and WARREN, H. (1984) *Something to Tell You*, London: Gay Teenager's Group.

VAN WICKLIN, J.F. (1984) 'Ego identity statuses: Addressing the continuum debate', Paper presented at the Annual Meeting of the Eastern Psychological Association, Baltimore, April 12–15.

VONDRACEK, F.W., SCHULENBERG, J., SKORIKOV, V., GILLESPIE, L.K. and WALHEIM, C. (1995) 'The relationship of identity status to career indecision during adolescence', *Journal of Adolescence*, **18**, pp. 17–29.

VYGOTSKY, L.S. (1962) *Thought and Language*, New York: Wiley.

WATERMAN, A.S. (1982) 'Identity development from adolescence to adulthood: An extension of theory and a review of research', *Developmental Psychology*, **18**, pp. 341–58.

WATERMAN, A.S. (Ed) (1985) *Identity in Adolescence: Processes and Contents*, San Francisco: Jossey-Bass.

WATERMAN, C.K. and NEVID, J.S. (1977) 'Sex differences in the resolution of the identity crisis', *Journal of Youth and Adolescence*, **6**, pp. 337–42.

WEINER, G. and ARNOT, M. (Ed) (1987) *Gender Under Scrutiny: New Inquiries in Education*, London: Unwin Hyman.

WELLINGS, K., FIELD, J., JOHNSON, A.M. and WADSWORTH, J. (1994) *Sexual Behaviour in Britain: The National Survey of Sexual Attitudes and Life Styles*, London: Penguin.

WILDEBLOOD, P. (1955) *Against the Law*, London: Weidenfeld and Nicolson.

WILLIS, P. (1977) *Learning to Labour: How Working Class Kids Get Working Class Jobs*, Aldershot: Gower.

WILLMOTT, P. (1969) *Adolescent Boys in the East End of London*, Harmondsworth: Penguin.

WINEFIELD, A.H., TIGGEMANN, M., WINEFIELD, H.R. and GOLDNEY, R.D. (1993) *Growing Up with Unemployment: A Longitudinal Study of Its Psychological Impact*, London: Routledge.

WINNICOTT, D.W. (1986) *Home is Where We Start From*, Harmondsworth: Penguin.

WOLFF, S. (1993) *Loners: The Life Paths of Unusual Children*, London: Routledge.

YOUNISS, J., McCLELLAN, J.A. and STROUSE, D. (1994) 'We're popular, but we're not snobs', in MONTEMAYOR, R., ADAMS, G.R. and GULLOTTA, T.P. (Eds) *Personal Relationships During Adolescence*, Thousand Oaks: Sage.

Index of Names

Subject Index